FREE TO CHOOSE

FREE TO CHOOSE

Decision making for Young Men

JOYCE SLAYTON MITCHELL

DELACORTE PRESS/NEW YORK

ACKNOWLEDGMENTS

Mai   rc Feigen
F   mpany.

by Warren Farrell: Adapted by
permission of Random House, Inc. from
THE LIBERATED MAN by Warren Farrell.
Copyright © 1974 by Warren Farrell.

Manufactured in the United States of America

First printing

Library of Congress Cataloging in Publication Data
Main entry under title:
Free to choose.

Includes bibliographies.
SUMMARY: Essays for young men about choices involving
sex, relationships, liberation, turning on, religion, athletics and
education.
1. Adolescent boys—Addresses, essays, lectures.
2. Decision making—Addresses, essays, lectures.
3. Boys—Conduct of life—Addresses, essays, lectures.
[1. Decision making.   2. Boys—Conduct of life.
3. Adolescence]   I. Mitchell, Joyce Slayton.
HQ797.F73   301.43'15   76-5589
ISBN 0-440-02723-3

Acknowledgments

It is with much admiration for the contributors that I thank each of them for their chapter. Each makes a very special contribution toward expanding the choices for a young man's decision making. My warmest thanks are extended to Roger Aubrey, Hal Boris, Doug Dillenbeck, Warren Farrell, Marc Fasteau, Marnin Kligfeld, Dick Lee, Art Montzka, Natalie Shepard, Len Swidler, and Betty Vetter.

The curriculum chapter was read by Grace Butterweck, counselor, Irvington High School in New York, and Rocco Orlando, professor, Southern Connecticut State College. My thanks to both of them for their expertise in curriculum and counseling but especially for their time and interest in this book.

I am grateful to the Reverend Patricia Budd Kepler, Harvard Divinity School, for our work together on the concept of spirituality. Also to Pat for her referral to Liz Rice, to whom I owe my thanks for help with the Eastern religions and meditation groups.

I want to thank Dr. Joseph H. Pleck of the University of Michigan, coauthor of *Men and Masculinity* and foremost leader in Men's Studies, for his sharing of ideas and bibliography.

To Warren Farrell, author of *The Liberated Man*, I owe special thanks for contributing three chapters. I am especially grateful to Warren for his ongoing dialogue with me about the concepts and issues of male liberation.

My appreciation goes to the many people at Dell who enthusiastically established a good working climate for *Free to Choose.*

It is a pleasure to thank Anne Hazelwood Brady for her friendship and her special editorial work on this book.

And thanks with love to my family—Bill, Elizabeth and Ned—for their contributions.

JSM
Wolcott, Vermont

FOR MY SON NED
WITH LOVE

Contributors

Roger F. Aubrey, director of guidance and health education, Brookline Public Schools, Massachusetts

Harold N. Boris, consultant in psychology, assistant clinical professor of psychiatry, Tufts University School of Medicine, Massachusetts

Douglas D. Dillenbeck, executive director of publications, College Entrance Examination Board, New York City

Warren Farrell, political scientist, author of *The Liberated Man*, New York City

Marc Feigen Fasteau, attorney, author of *The Male Machine*, New York City

Marnin Kligfeld, Ph.D. candidate in counseling psychology, University of Southern California, Los Angeles

Richard V. Lee, physician, associate professor of medicine, director of medical clinics, Yale University School of Medicine, Connecticut

Arthur Montzka, high school music teacher and photographer, Sycamore, Illinois

Joyce Slayton Mitchell, consultant in education, Wolcott, Vermont

Natalie M. Shepard, professor emeritus, Denison University, Ohio

Leonard Swidler, professor of religion, Temple University, Philadelphia

Betty M. Vetter, director, Scientific Manpower Commission, Washington D.C.

Contents

An Introduction

BOYS WILL BE BOYS*

BY MARC FEIGEN FASTEAU

* Adapted from Marc Feigen Fasteau, *The Male Machine* (New York: McGraw-Hill, 1974). Adapted and printed with permission of the author and publisher.

Families prefer boys. It's a boy! is followed by great joy and some relief. Boys are the heirs to the family name and the better qualified heir to the family property and interests. "Boys carry on the family name," "We wanted a boy first," "Boys are easier to raise," and "The money we spend on a boy's education really counts," say the parents.

Schools prefer boys. Out of 2760 elementary school stories from 134 textbooks published recently by 14 major publishing companies, a study in New Jersey found that there were only 2 girl-centered stories for every 5 boy-centered ones, that there were 147 different adult role possibilities for boys while only 25 for girls, and in the 67 stories in which one sex demeaned the other, *65 of these were directed against girls!*

Churches and synagogues prefer boys. Boys grow up to be men, who are the only qualified ones to hold the top job . . . priest or rabbi. And the Protestant minister whose church is filled with women and children says, "We need more people for leaders in our church." More people to him doesn't mean more women and children —it means more men.

Boys prefer boys. In a study of eight- and eleven-year-old boys psychologist Ruth Hartley asked what boys need to know: "[Boys] should know what girls don't know—how to climb, how to make a fire, how to carry things; they should have more ability than girls; they need to know how to stay out of trouble; they need to know arithmetic and spelling more than girls do."

The home, church, or synagogue, and school: the three basic institutions that socialize young children into their expected role in our society are all teaching sexism. That is, male is normal. And male is better. It's hard to live in a world of boys and girls and women and men if you are raised with contempt for girls and women.

When you learn your lesson well—that boys really count more than girls—there is no way for you to be friends with a girl now nor the possibility for you to have an equal relationship later. Stereotypes work. But you can learn to break out of them as you trust your own version of you—and all you are meant to be.

Marc Feigen Fasteau wrote one of the first male liberation books, *The Male Machine*. An adaptation from his book, "Boys Will Be Boys" helps you to see the roots of the trouble—the way boys have been programmed to sexism. Mr. Fasteau is also a lawyer who practices law in New York City in partnership with his attorney wife.

Boys Will Be Boys

BY MARC FEIGEN FASTEAU

Jeffrey, a friend's son, is seven years old and likes a girl of the same age who lives in his apartment building. But when he learned that she was going to transfer to his school, he got an agitated look on his face. "It'll spoil everything," he said. And it nearly has. The other boys in his class tease him and beat him up if they see him playing with her. Things got so bad that one day, when his mother came to school to walk Jeffrey and his friend back to his house so they could play together, the girl, without a word, carefully walked ten yards behind so the other boys wouldn't think Jeffrey was going to play with her. When she and Jeffrey had a fight, her ultimate act of betrayal was to tell the boys that she and Jeffrey had sleep-over dates. She knew he would catch hell from them.

In a second-grade class I visited, I asked the boys whether they played with the girls. Obviously expecting approval, they told me proudly that they didn't. One was embarrassed enough to start a fight when the other boys accused him of liking a particular girl.

A subscriber to *Ms.* magazine, in a letter to the editor, described a scene in which a five-year-old boy was being teased by four other boys of about the same age. Unable to endure any more, pushed to the point of tearful rage, he turned to the leader of the group and, with a look of pure hatred, screamed the most horrible insult he could think of: "You girl!"

Little boys put down little girls so much that it becomes what we expect of them. A "girls—yuk!" line is a standard part of family-style television comedies involving boys who get sympathy on the program from the grown men. The "funny story" at the end of a CBS network news broadcast one night, for example, was how a twelve-year-old had won a championship horseshoe-pitching match in which his thirteen-year-old brother had also competed. The twelve-year-old had provoked the older boy, who had responded by hitting him, and injuring his own throwing hand, thus hampering his performance the next day. How had the victor precipitated the fight? asked the newscaster. Cut to filmed interview with the kid: "I called him a girl," he said, and he grinned the grin of someone who thinks he has done something expected and amusing. Cut back to matching grin of comfortable male complicity from the newscaster as he says, ". . . and good night from CBS News."

It is wishful thinking to believe that this kind of hostility toward females is merely a passing phase that somehow disappears with time. It is not. Elaborated and layered over with other feelings, *it is the key to the way adult men feel about women.* Let us look at its roots.

As early as ages four and five, reports psychologist Ruth Hartley, boys learn what is expected of them as males and restrict themselves to what they believe are things boys should do. What this means in large part is not being like a girl, or, what is the same thing, not being a "sissy." A few years later, they are quite capable of expanding on this point. Eight- and eleven-year-old boys in a study of sex-role pressures on male children, by Hartley, described girls in these terms:

> They have to stay close to the house; they are expected to play quietly and be gentler than boys; they are often afraid; they must not be rough; they have to keep clean; they cry when they are scared or hurt; they are afraid to go to rough places like rooftops and empty lots; their activities consist of

"fopperies" like playing with dolls, fussing over babies and sitting and talking about dresses; they need to know how to cook, sew, and take care of children, but spelling and arithmetic are not as important for them as for boys.

This image of girls, reeking of limitations and restraint, is not just the product of parents' and friends' expectations. Our schools also do their share in training boys to be boys. For example, Virginia Kidd writes in *Now You See* that California's first-grade reading text, published by Harper and Row, paints this picture of girls and their proper relationship to boys:

> [Mark and Janet are brother and sister. Janet gets new skates. She tries them and falls.]
> "Mark! Janet!" said Mother. "What is going on here?"
> "She cannot skate," said Mark. "I can help her. I want to help her. Look at her, Mother. Just look at her. She is just like a girl. She gives up."
> [Mother forces Janet to try again.]
> "Now you see," said Mark. "Now you can skate. But just with me to help you."
> [Janet, needless to say, never makes a similar remark to Mark.]

This is not unusual. A survey of their commonly used children's textbooks by Marjorie B. U'Ren in *The Image of Women in Textbooks* showed females were described more often than males as lazy and incapable of direct action as well as more likely to give up easily, collapse in tears, betray secrets, and act on petiy or selfish motives. Nearly all of the adult female characters (and only 4 percent of all of the adults were women) were shown as assistants to men. Madame Curie, for example, appeared as little more than a helpmate to her husband and another male scientist. Among the descriptions of present-day professionals there was only one working female, a scientist. The three other male scientists in the same chapter are shown working alone on projects demanding originality and exacting mental effort, while the text and picture caption for the woman scientist state that she is not working independently and that the idea she is testing was assigned to her by others. Given this picture of females, it is not surprising that the boys in the Hartley study described their own characteristics as the exact opposite from girls':

> [Boys] have to be able to fight in case a bully comes along; they have to be athletic; they have to be able to run fast; they must be able to play rough games; they need to know how to play many games—curbball, baseball, basketball, football; they need to be smart; they need to be able to take care of themselves; they should know what girls don't know—how to climb, how to make a fire, how to carry things; they should have more ability than girls; they need to know how to stay out of trouble; they need to know arithmetic and spelling more than girls do.

The "not like a girl" aspects of being a boy come out even more clearly in the answers to Hartley's question, "What is expected of boys?" which gets at the kinds of boys' behavior expected and approved by grown-ups.

> Boys believe grown-ups expect them to be noisy; to get dirty; to mess up the house; to be naughty; to be "outside" more than girls are; not to be crybabies; not to be "softies," not to be "behind" like girls are; and to get into trouble more than girls do. Moreover, boys are not allowed to do the kind of things that girls usually do, but girls may do the kind of things that boys do.

The situation is practically perfect for causing anxiety. The idea toward which a boy's parents and friends pressure him is not clear, defined as much by what he should *not* do and be as by what is approved, and, most important, calling for a boy to hide his feelings and to hide his needs for others.

Fathers, believing in a slightly more grown-up version of the same thing, try to conceal from their sons their feelings and their dependencies, thereby passing on the same dehumanized image of masculinity. The result, Hartley says, is "an overstraining to be masculine, a virtual panic at being caught doing anything traditionally defined as feminine, and hostility toward anything even hinting at 'femininity,' including females themselves."

Boys want so desperately to be different from girls that anything that appears to close the gap, any similarity in behavior that they are aware of, is frightening. My neighborhood tree-house gang, for example, arranged the foot- and handholds leading up to our tree house so "no girls can get up there." There were no secret male rituals we wanted to indulge in; it just made us feel different and more manly to keep girls out.

Of course, boys don't see the male and female roles as merely different. To be a boy—prospectively a man —is clearly superior. Although many girls want for a period of time to be boys and do their best to act like boys (so many in fact that we have a word—*tomboy*— to describe them), very few boys want to be girls according to Inge Broverman, et al., in "Sex-Role Stereotypes: A Current Appraisal," *Journal of Social Issues*. Naturally, they project these differences into the future. The boys in Hartley's study thought grown women are, among other things, fearful, indecisive, stay-at-homes, physically weak, squeamish about seeing blood, unadventurous, more easily hurt and killed than men, and afraid of getting wet or getting an electric shock. They thought that women "have a way of doing things the wrong way," that they scream instead of taking charge in emergencies, fuss over children's grades, and very easily become jealous and envy their husbands (although it is conceded that they make their children feel good). Of women's traditional activities they said,

"They are always at those crazy household
duties and don't have time for anything else."
"Their work is just regular drudging." "Women do
things like cooking and washing and sewing because that's all they can do." "Women haven't
enough strength in the head or in the body to do
most jobs."

By contrast, they thought that grown men had to be
strong to protect women and children in emergencies,
do rough, dirty, and unpleasant work, earn money, care
for their children, and get along with their wives, and
that they get tired a lot. On the positive side, however,
men are usually in charge of things, they mess up the
house, "mostly do what they want to do," decide how
to spend the money, and get first choice of the most
comfortable chair. Although they get mad a lot, they
laugh and make jokes more than women. They are
more fun to be with than mothers, more exciting to have
around, and they have the best ideas. With this vision
of the future, what boy or girl would not choose the
male role with its responsibilities, decision-making
power, and first choice on everything?

Girls and boys notice these differences very early.
My kindergarten informant, a self-assured girl of five,
reported how it was when the boys and girls played
Red Light-Green Light-One-Two-Three together. Do
you remember the game? The leader of the game stands
at the front of the room, with eyes covered, and says
"Red Light-Green Light-One-Two-Three" as fast as
possible, while the other players try to move up as
close to the front of the room as they can. When the
leader opens her or his eyes, any player still moving
has to go back to the starting line. My informant reported that the boys would readily go back to the
starting line when caught by a boy leader but that when
she or another girl was the leader, they would refuse to
go back. In her case, one came up, pushed her aside,
and, restoring the natural order of things, pronounced
himself the leader.

In adult life, expression of these attitudes may be indirect because of sexual attraction, the demands of family life, and social disapproval of open hostility to women. But, underneath, they remain, reinforced through the years by our families, schools, and churches, and our culture, shaping nearly every aspect of men's adult relationships with women, and never to be outgrown.

It is extremely difficult to separate out the biological influences from the cultural influences on the development of sex roles and identity because, according to M. Lewis in "Parents and Children: Sex Role Development," boys are treated differently from girls beginning at birth. During the first two years, for example, mothers talk to and smile at girl babies more than boy babies. Boys are touched—kissed, hugged, and rocked —more for the first six months, but after that they are touched less than girls. Beginning when boy babies are six months old, mothers are more likely to discourage them than girls from seeking physical contact by picking them up and facing them away or by distracting their attention with objects of some kind, probably out of a belief that it is more important for boys to learn to be on their own.

Historically, the traditional sex roles must have grown out of practical arrangements necessary to child-bearing in primitive societies. Women were either nursing infants or pregnant much of their adult lives, conditions which limited their mobility, while hunting game for food resulted in men going away from the home. A division of labor in which women stayed at home and took care of the children and men went out and hunted made sense. The greater physical strength of men may also have had something to do with their primacy within the primitive family: without a more highly developed social structure and technology, the threat of superior physical force is one of the effective means of establishing dominance and control.

Today, the male/female division of labor, with all its complicated psychological, political, economic, and cultural elaborations, is obsolete. What males can do and what females can do has little to do with physical strength and speed of foot. In America today these attributes are not of central importance. Women spend only a small part of their lives bearing children and, for most of that period, may continue in their regular careers and responsibilities.

Because socially significant masculine and feminine behavior patterns are not biologically determined, men and women often act in a way that society says is reserved for the other sex. Keeping the stereotypes straight can be a difficult task for the traditionalist. "The base of male conceit," according to Norman Mailer in "The Prisoner of Sex," *Harper's Magazine*, is "that men [can] live with truths too unsentimental for women." But in a study conducted by William Kephart of the University of Pennsylvania, it was found that over a lifetime the America male becomes infatuated and falls in love more often than the female, while women see their boyfriends' faults more clearly and are much less driven by romantic compulsions. In other words, what we say is masculine behavior, and what men actually do may be two different kinds of behavior.

For the most part, men handle the problem of keeping their masculine behavior straight by acting opposite of what they think is feminine behavior. When men are in doubt they fall back on describing women as the opposite of what they, as individuals, think they are like, and even as the opposite of what they are like at any given moment. This device, needless to say, is used unconsciously, allowing the speaker to maintain an image of himself as consistent, an important masculine trait.

But if the twists and turns of definition as to what behavior can be considered masculine and what feminine can sometimes be obscure, the basic attitudes about sex roles—the teaching that boys will be boys— come through loud and clear. First, we—men and women both—believe in the either/or theory of human personality even if we do not always conform to it: a person who is tough is always tough; a person who is tender and soft is always tender and soft; we do not expect people to be tough in one situation and tender in another according to the demands of the occasion, to have both responses in their repertoires. Second, men believe that to be masculine they have to be radically different from women. Third, men believe they are better than women and that, in order to retain their masculine self-image when they deal with women, they must dominate and outperform them in every area except child rearing, homemaking, amateur culture, and the management of social life. Fourth, the areas assigned to women are thought of as less important and difficult than those assigned to men, and men, to keep their masculine identification and status, try to stay out of them.

WHO CHOOSES?

WHO CHOOSES?

A Person Is Free to Choose

BY JOYCE SLAYTON MITCHELL

Many teachers, counselors, and parents act as if they know who you will be and what you should choose. You should take a strong academic program with a lot of mathematics and science leading to a profession or business career that makes a lot of money or has high prestige. Of course, they say, everyone is different and an individual, but when it comes to advice, the male stereotype is usually in back of their heads. Most educators assume that a young man will put his career first; his friendships and marriage don't count as much to him and will just fall into place. If a man's work life goes really well he won't be bothered by poor personal relationships anyway. The assumption is that you are going to be in the role of achiever/provider rather than a person who can choose to integrate your personal life and your work life.

When you begin to see yourself developing as a whole person with many choices rather than as a man who has to earn more money than anyone else, who has to control and dominate relationships, and who has to stay cool while competing with his peers, then you will work through your own values to develop a life-style of your own. You will begin to rely more on your own experiences and feelings of self-discovery—and less on the cultural expectations for boys.

Free to Choose is designed as a handbook for dis-

covering all the things you are and can be before you
are free to choose. A person discovers what he is like
and then decides what he will do about it. This book
will help you to decide.

Good decisions are made when you have yourself
altogether as an integrated person. There isn't anything
about you that can be separated out of your life as if
it isn't related to your decisions. Your sexuality, schoolwork, and your friendships, your spirituality and your
summertime—all count as you are learning to become
a person who is *Free to Choose*.

MORE INFORMATION FOR BECOMING A PERSON

Many men are working toward freeing themselves
and their brothers from the male stereotype. Men's
studies courses, men's resource centers, and men's con-
ferences are beginning to be organized. Professor
Joseph H. Pleck of the University of Michigan has col-
lected men's resources and has published current lists
of men's organizations and publications. With other
men, Pleck has started a Men's Awareness Network,
where you can write for up-to-date information about
meetings, publications, and resources. For the Men's
Awareness Network newsletter write Knoxville Men's
Resource Center, P.O. Box 8060, University Station,
Knoxville, Tenn. 37916. $1.00.

For more information read the following basic male
liberation books:

Farrell, Warren. *The Liberated Man*. New York:
Random House, 1974; New York: Bantam, 1975.
Fasteau, Marc Feigen. *The Male Machine*. New
York: McGraw Hill, 1974.
Nichols, Jack. *Men's Liberation*. New York: Pen-
guin, 1975.
Pleck, Joseph, and Sawyer, Jack, eds. *Men and Mas-
culinity*. Englewood Cliffs, N.J.: Prentice-Hall,
1974.

SEXUAL CHOICES

Learning
and Deciding About Sex

"How am I supposed to treat a liberated woman?" asked a young man in a liberation workshop. "I like to look at her body, I want her to know that I admire her sexually, but I don't want to offend her." "How can I enjoy a woman's body and not come off as if I'm treating her as a sex object?" "To be treated as a sex object—as if that is all I am—*is* offensive to me," was the response of a thoughtful woman. "But to treat me as a sexual being as part of my totality—just as I appreciate your sexuality as an interesting part of you—is not offensive."

Looking at women as sex objects—and nothing more—is what liberated women object to. It's the same narrowness as when females look at males as success objects. Instead of seeing him as a total person, they see only his career, or prestige, or his income; and with younger men, their potential for being a success. But a young person is a sexual being and something more. A young person is successful and something more.

The problem for men in treating women as sex objects is that it puts men in constant competition with other men to be ready at all times to perform sexually. Making it with a woman is so competitive that this readiness to perform at all times is one reason why men retreat and segregate themselves from women, according to Marc Feigen Fasteau, author of *The Male Machine*.

One way to get out of this constant competition "to be on the make"—this false measure of a "real" man— is to integrate your understanding about your sexuality with everything else about you. Especially the kinds of friendships you want right now and how these friendships support or don't support you, encourage or don't encourage you.

Dr. Richard V. Lee, Director of Medical Clinics at Yale University School of Medicine, details the specific facts about physical maturity, intercourse, pregnancy, contraception, abortion, venereal disease, and homosexuality. Dr. Lee writes that "adolescents who regard intercourse as a necessity use sex as a substitute for intimacy and love." "Sexual intercourse," he says, "should be a choice, never a necessity!"

Dr. Lee has counseled many young men who have completely rejected their parents' values and morals the minute they arrived on the Yale campus. Some of these young men take on a whole new set of peer morals before they think about who they are and what they stand for. "It takes time to work through your own sexual morals," says Dr. Lee, "and substituting peer values for parents' values still doesn't make them your own."

This chapter will help you learn about sex and then to think through where you are on your sexual values— so that you will be *Free to Choose.*

Learning
and Deciding About Sex*

BY RICHARD V. LEE, M.D.

Learning about sex is a process often clouded by mis-
information, embarrassment, myth, fantasy, and taboo.
For a number of reasons your parents, or adults close
to you, may find it difficult to talk to you about it.
Sometimes they hold back out of ignorance or fear,
sometimes because they do not want you to have too
much information too early, sometimes because they
find it painful to share their deepest intimacies and disappointments with anyone, but mostly because they
care about you and realize that you, too, are going to
have to make your own discoveries, in your own time,
in your own way.

Sex is a word that can have many meanings. Usually
it means the biology of reproduction, behavioral psychology, and a hodgepodge of related items and ideas.
More specifically, the word sex refers to the biologic
facts of life—the anatomy of sexual organs and how
they work. Sexuality can also refer to more than the
ways the sexual organs are used, and include your view
of yourself, and the ways you respond to and care for
others.

* Thanks to M. J. Gray, M.D., whose chapter "Deciding
About Sex" in *Other Choices for Becoming a Woman* (New
York: Dell, 1975) served as a model.

PUBERTY IN BOYS

To begin with, you were born with your own innate and essentially unchangeable schedule for growth. In the process of maturation (barring illness, malnutrition, or congenital abnormalities) you will enter the stage of growth called puberty, the time when many physical changes take place in your body.

Accepting these changes, and the sexual feelings and impulses that accompany them, is complicated because you don't know when to expect which changes. For example, a friend may grow a heavy growth of pubic hair without a change in the range of his voice; another may grow over six feet tall without his penis getting any larger. If you are embarrassed by the slow rate of change in your body, no amount of wishing will make it happen faster or make the waiting easier. Not only will you worry if maturity is ever going to happen, but you will worry if it is happening normally. Several embarrassing or worrisome things can occur during this time. One is the appearance of erections of the penis without any warning, at the wrong time or with hardly anything appearing to cause it. Although rarely ever noticed by people around you, you are keenly aware of your erect penis. Fortunately, these erections go away as quickly as they appear. You may, while asleep, experience erections, sometimes ejaculations or "wet dreams"; also acne and enlargement of breasts are normal during adolescence.

The first signs of sexual development in a boy are enlargement of the testicles and the appearance of pubic hair. They usually begin between the ages of eleven and fifteen, but there is a wide range of normal differences. Special cells within the testicles secrete hormones which are essential for the development of what are called secondary sex characteristics. Under the influence of these hormones, pubic hair grows, the penis enlarges, underarm hair appears, and the voice begins to change. Also at this time the testicles begin to make sperm and the boy begins to have ejaculations.

Sperm are self-propelling cells capable of penetrating and fertilizing an egg. They are transported from the testicle stored in a reservoir called the seminal vesicles. The semen which contains the sperm is ejaculated through the same tubing through which the urine passes. The semen ejaculated contains about two hundred million sperm cells. Because no urine can pass out of the bladder during an erection, there is never any urine in the semen. Most adolescent males will experience enlargement of the breasts. This may be symmetrical, involve only one breast, or one more than the other and cause some sensitivity to the area. Again, this is a common and normal occurrence which may worry you even though breast enlargement is always temporary. Furthermore both boys and girls frequently develop acne during or soon after puberty. Like unwanted erections, unwanted pimples are almost always more noticeable to you than to the rest of the world. In almost all cases, the condition clears up. Similarly, both boys and girls will notice increased perspiration odors as sweat and oil glands mature during puberty.

MASTURBATION

Most adolescents are surprised by the sudden upsurge of sexual feelings and impulses. The eruptions of intense sexual thoughts and stimulation may produce **pleasure or guilt and frequently both.** Being "turned on" by seeing your older sister in her underwear, "falling in love" twice in one day with a different person, having erotic daydreams, masturbating and feeling guilty about it, are all part of normal development. It takes time to get to know yourself.

Like everything else having to do with normal sexual development, most adolescents masturbate. Studies have shown that 90 percent of adolescent boys masturbate. The stimulation of one's own genitals is one of the most prevalent sexual acts, yet it is surrounded by fable and fantasy. Boys hear that masturbation gives them acne, makes them insane, will make hair grow on their hands, damages their penises, or will render them unable to father a child. There is *no* evidence that masturbation does anything more than provide a release from sexual tension, reduce the drive momentarily for sexual activity, and increase guilt feelings in those who think it is wrong. Indeed, masturbation or "jerking off" is usually the first voluntary experience of ejaculation for young men. Stimulation of the penis produces rising rhythmic muscular contractions climaxing in the ejaculation of semen. The release of physical and emotional tension following sexual stimulation is called a climax or orgasm. Regardless of whether this occurs as a result of masturbation, petting, or sexual intercourse, there is no difference physiologically between an orgasm produced by masturbation or by sexual intercourse. Emotionally, there is a wide variety of difference, depending on the circumstances, state of well-being, and state of health of the person or persons involved. This is particularly true of women.

PUBERTY IN GIRLS

With your new awareness of your own body and its changes, and of your own feelings and impulses, it is natural for you to wonder about the changes taking place in girls of your age.

Girls generally mature sexually before boys, sometime between the ages of nine and fourteen, but with considerable variation. Usually the first sign of puberty is the growth of pubic and underarm hair caused by hormones from the adrenal glands. Soon after, estrogen, the chief female hormone, starts the breasts to grow. It takes a few years for the breasts to develop. There is no relationship between breast size and the ability to produce milk, following childbirth, in later years.

These developmental changes are accompanied by changes in appearance of the external genitals, or vulva, and changes in the internal sexual organs. Continued production of hormones by the ovaries results in the growth of the uterus and causes the lining of the uterus to become thicker and suitable for an egg to implant if one is fertilized. If pregnancy does not occur, the level of estrogen temporarily drops, the lining of the uterus breaks down, and blood appears at the opening of the vagina, the beginning of the first menstrual period. Thereafter, a cyclic pattern is set up, usually menstruating every twenty-six to thirty-two days. About twelve to sixteen days after the beginning of a menstrual period, an egg is released by the ovary. This is picked up by the end of the Fallopian tube which carries the egg to the uterus. If the egg is fertilized along the way, the egg will implant itself on the uterine lining and the fetus will begin to grow. If pregnancy does not occur, the egg disintegrates, estrogen levels drop, and another menstrual period begins.

A number of myths and misconceptions exist regarding menstruation. It is still all too common to hear it referred to as "the curse" or "falling of the roof." Periods are an outward sign of normal function, accompanied, though not always, by some discomfort or "cramps" which in some cases may be severe but in most cases are minor. Each woman has her own cycle and her own variations; rarely is it exactly twenty-eight days.

As with boys, sexual feelings increase with sexual maturation. Many girls release sexual tension by stimulation of the clitoris, an erectile organ with sexual sensitivity similar to the penis and located above the vaginal opening. As with boys, masturbation by girls does not cause physical or mental harm, and may often be the first voluntary experience with orgasm. Orgasm in girls consists of rhythmic vaginal contractions and release of emotional and physical tension and may vary widely in intensity. During stimulation of the genitals and other sensitive areas of the body, a thick fluid lubricates the vaginal walls. Though the sex organs are very different, recent studies demonstrate many similarities between the female and male sexual response.

SEXUAL INTERCOURSE

Sexual intercourse has been traditionally defined as an erect penis entering a vagina, a rather clinical but physiologically accurate description. However, it is an inadequate definition, which ignores the personhood of the two people involved, and fails to recognize that the end result of an act of sexual intercourse may result in bringing another life into the world. Ideally, it should be described as a coming together sexually with communication paramount.

Orgasm does not automatically occur as a result of intercourse. Most women are sensitive to the circumstances in which intercourse takes place and in the quality of the total experience. These women do not always respond during their early sexual experiences. Many women require time to develop the confidence, trust, and relaxation necessary to make intercourse a good experience, whereas men are often less sensitive to the circumstances in which intercourse takes place. Moreover, the male's sexual response often occurs more rapidly than the female's. A penis can become erect very quickly, and orgasm with ejaculation is possible even before the woman is aroused.

Impatience at this time often causes discomfort and destroys the pleasure of sexual intercourse. Discomfort to the woman is usually due to lack of vaginal lubrication and relaxation of the vaginal muscles which may be due to anxiety or impatience on the part of her partner. The hymen, a partial membrane around the vaginal opening in women who have not had intercourse, is easily stretched by tampons, athletics, and sexual foreplay, and is rarely the cause of discomfort.

A lot of emphasis has been placed on orgasm. Young people may feel obliged to have an orgasm with every sexual experience. Many may feel guilty if they do not elicit orgasm or multiple orgasms in a partner. Multiple orgasms and orgasm every time are not the only aspects of satisfying sexual needs. Sexual relations are not a job or a competitive sport. Mutual pleasure and respect are infinitely more important. It takes time to learn how to make love.

CONTRACEPTION

Without birth control 80 percent of normal women having intercourse regularly will become pregnant within a year. Pregnancy occurs when one of the millions of sperm reaches an egg ready to be fertilized. Even if the semen is deposited on the outside of the vagina, pregnancy is possible. The fertilized egg implants itself on the wall of the uterus and begins to grow, producing the placenta, umbilical cord, and the fetus (all fetuses are undifferentiated until the seventh week when differences in sex begin to form) which usually takes nine months to mature into a baby ready for life outside the womb. After about six weeks from the first day of the last menstrual period, it is possible to tell if a woman is pregnant by measuring one of the hormones produced by the placenta and excreted in the urine. Urine tests for pregnancy are simple, reliable, and readily available.

The decision to practice birth control and the decision to have a baby should be arrived at by mutual consent of both partners. The man who persuades a woman to have unprotected sexual intercourse without any thought about paternity is disregarding his responsibility to life.

Contraception is especially important for the woman because she is the one who gets pregnant, and because the method of contraception selected has implications for her health. The three most effective methods of birth control designed for women are the pill, IUD, and the diaphragm. Both the pill and an IUD (a device placed by a doctor through the opening of the uterus)

have known side effects. It has also been shown that
the use of birth control pills is dangerous enough to
cause death in some women susceptible to blood-
clotting. None of the methods is foolproof. So far, for
men, the condom, a simple rubber sheath placed over
the penis, and available without a doctor's prescription
in any drugstore, is the best protection against impreg-
nating a woman or in transferring, or in contracting, a
venereal disease. The condom, when used in combination with the diaphragm and with a vaginal spermicidal
foam (also available without prescription, though the
diaphragm must be fitted by a doctor), has been proved
in recent studies to be as effective as the IUD. Most
of the other methods should be mentioned only to say
that they do not work well. *Rhythm* (intercourse only
on non-ovulating days) is particularly unreliable to
the teenager whose periods may vary. Pregnancies
have been documented on every day of the menstrual
cycle, and even with those whose periods are very
regular, there are frequent failures. *Douching* (washing out the vagina) should be mentioned only to
condemn it, since the sperm start at the cervix and
travel out of reach in seconds. Makeshift plastic and
Saran wrap condoms are not at all safe. *Withdrawal*
(pulling the penis out before ejaculation) requires
more control than most young men possess and frequently leaves the woman unsatisfied.

Abstinence from sexual intercourse is also an option.
Not having sexual intercourse is common to a great
many friendships. Anyone who insists on sexual intercourse as a prerequisite for friendship or affection is
practicing emotional and sexual blackmail.

UNWANTED PREGNANCIES

Some pregnancies end before three or four months because the fetus is not developing as it should. This is
called spontaneous abortion. When the pregnancy is
ended by removal of the fetus from the uterus by a

doctor, it is called induced abortion. When the pregnancy is ended by the act of a nonphysician, it is called criminal abortion.

Although it is now possible for a woman to have a legal, induced abortion under the best conditions, abortions are not as safe as not being pregnant. They are expensive, involve some health risk, and cause stress even though the woman chooses it. Women may also be subjected to humiliation, guilt, and/or shame because of the objections of some religious and ethical groups to abortion.

Another alternative to unwanted pregnancies is to carry the fetus to term, and after birth, release the baby for adoption. This may exert a heavy emotional toll on the mother and child for years to come. Since the male has almost none of the long-term ill effects of irresponsible sexual behavior, it is not surprising that an arrogant and cavalier attitude toward sex and women may develop among adolescent and young adult men. Sex may become something of a "con game," with the woman as the mark; and the boy "can't lose." In a mature and loving relationship an unwanted pregnancy will be rare. Unless such a relationship exists, and there is a clear recognition of future responsibilities, marriage is seldom a good idea for adolescents or young adults even though the woman is pregnant. The divorce rate in shotgun marriages is about 75 percent and the toll in unhappiness and unwanted babies continues.

Despite the best intentions, unwanted pregnancies occur. If you are the father or are named the father, then seek the advice of another responsible adult you trust. Your parents obviously won't be very happy about it, but most of the time you will be pleasantly surprised by their ability to deal with your honesty and to help you through difficulties. As distressing as it may seem, when you know you are the father, try to talk with the young woman's parents. They may be bitter and angry, but may also acknowledge your maturity and willingness to accept responsibility. Most important—talk with the young woman. After all, you got into the situation together, and you should try to handle the problem together even though you don't get married.

VENEREAL DISEASE

Venereal diseases are infections transmitted from one person to another by the skin-to-skin contact that occurs during sexual intercourse. The three most common of these diseases are gonorrhea, syphilis, and genital herpes simplex infection. Every case of venereal disease means at least two other people are infected. The young man, from whom a woman catches gonorrhea, got his infection from someone else. It is imperative, therefore, that he see a physician for diagnosis and treatment if he thinks he may be infected. It is equally imperative that he cooperate with his doctor or the public health authorities in diagnosing and treating his sexual partner, by having her come for treatment to his or her doctor or to appropriate authorities.

Second only to the common cold, gonorrhea, known colloquially as "GC" or "the clap," is the most prevalent of all communicable diseases in the United States. The infection commonly produces no symptoms in women. When women do notice symptoms, they complain of vaginal discharge and burning on urination. In men, infection produces a discharge or pus from the penis and considerable burning and pain with urination. Symptoms usually begin two to six days after exposure. Gonorrhea can be treated with penicillin under a doctor's care. Untreated, the disease can have serious consequences.

Syphilis is unusual because it can persist in the body for many years without causing symptoms until critical damage has been done to vital organs, such as the brain and the heart. The first sign of the disease is a sore, the primary chancre, which occurs on the exposed body part, usually two to three weeks after exposure. It is generally not tender, and is more often noted on the penis than in the vagina or on the cervix. Micro-organisms are spread throughout the body by the bloodstream. About the time the primary sore has healed, a scaly rash appears all over the body, but especially on the palm and soles. This secondary rash will heal spontaneously, and the patient will have no symptoms until many years later when treatment is no longer effective. Because syphilis can go unnoticed so easily, it is a good idea to have a blood test if you suspect you may have a venereal disease. Almost all states require a syphilis blood test prior to marriage and during a pregnancy.

Herpes simplex infections of genitals are caused by a virus that causes cold sores. The sores can be on the penis or on the skin of the groin, but most commonly it infects the cervix (the opening to the uterus). There is no cure for herpes simplex sores. They heal spontaneously and usually occur only once. Unfortunately a few people suffer recurrent episodes.

HOMOSEXUALITY

Since adolescence is a time for exploration and experimentation, with physical and emotional changes developing, sexual experimentation between members of the same sex sometimes occurs. This is usually a passing stage of development. In the course of growing up, friendships with boys are supplemented by friendships with girls which arouse feelings leading to a deepening relationship.

Our society has tended to divide itself into an either/or view of sexuality which doesn't usually work because most people are not all one or the other. In the late 1940s a clearer view was put forth by the well-known biologist Dr. A. C. Kinsey and others who described sexual behavior on a line ranging from "exclusively heterosexual" (preferring sexual relationships with a member of the opposite sex) to "exclusively homosexual" (preferring sexual relationships with the same sex), with varying degrees in between. A person's place on the line is based on his or her sexual activity, which, for most people, will include varying frequencies of and interest in both homosexual and heterosexual behavior. One or even several homosexual acts do not necessarily mean that you will have an exclusively homosexual orientation as an adult. In the same way, a person who has had one or several heterosexual experiences is not necessarily uninterested in homosexual ones. It may be reassuring to know that many men and women have had homosexual relationships in early adolescence and later established heterosexual relationships as well. Furthermore, there is no certain way of predicting from adolescent behavior what a boy's sexual orientation will be as an adult. Some people appear to function either in heterosexual or homosexual relationships, and they are considered bisexual. In addition, the term homosexual is sometimes misapplied to people who do not conform to society's stereotype of what a man (or a woman) should look and act like.

People view homosexuality in different ways. Some consider it an illness; others regard it as immoral and illegal; still others view it as a natural relationship. Whatever the view, there remain many legal and strongly disapproving restrictions that discriminate against homosexuals in education, the awarding of scholarships, employment, housing, and family and social life. This intolerance has often led to serious and tragic emotional problems.

Worries about sexuality often seem to take over our whole life. Worries about homosexuality seem even worse. If you are concerned about the possibility that you may be inclined to prefer a sexual relationship with another young man, seek out an older friend whom you trust to discuss the matter with you. Just the idea of talking with someone often puts the problem in perspective. Sexuality, even though it is central to our lives, is not everything we are. Keeping our sexual preferences in perspective with everything else that is a part of us—intellect, creativity, values, and goals for now

and for the future—often helps in coping with these
crucial concerns.

MORALS, MARRIAGE, AND MANNERS

Learning to accept and control sexual feelings and
sexual behavior is a crucial task. Outside of the meaningful codes of behavior in marriage is the concept of
"premature sex." Studies have shown that sexual intercourse occurring early in a relationship produces dis-
tresses greater than the immature can handle and often
accelerates the breakup of the couple. Love, trust, and
commitments are needed in all sexual relations. Good
lovemaking and especially sexual intercourse take time
and patience. Without a special relationship, learning
to make love can be an embarrassing, devastating experience for one or both partners. Nor is the formality of
marriage a guarantee of successful sexual relations in
the absence of this special kind of relationship. Even
marriages can be premature. The risk of divorce is 50
percent when two teenagers marry and 75 percent if
the young woman is already pregnant. Premature involvement may result in curtailed education, reduced
life goals, and unexpected physical and emotional risks.
The earlier you become involved, the further you go
sexually, and the more compromises you make with
other important matters such as education and jobs, the
more it hurts when you break up.

Intercourse can be one of the greatest or one of the
loneliest, most hurtful experiences a person can have. It
is not a cure-all; indeed it can be used as a form of rebellion, revenge, or exploitation, hurting not only your
partner and yourself, but others as well. There is a
tremendous difference between desirability and necessity. Necessary sex becomes an obligation and very
quickly a burden for at least one of the couple. Desir-
able sex is a shared pleasure, appreciated for its making
the relationship stronger, not because it satisfies only
selfish needs.

You may well ask how you go about making these seemingly earth-shattering decisions. What guidelines do you look for? Talking about premarital precautions and physiology will not tell you much about pride, modesty, shame, or codes of behavior. The best sex information in the world, while contributing to your decisions, cannot make those decisions for you.

What can you do to find out where you stand? You can ask these questions of yourself. Work them out with your friends—maybe even your parents would like to know what kinds of answers are meaningful to you. The answers you give can help you clarify your approach to sex, morals, and manners. Some of the most important questions and the reasons for asking them are:

1. Does a sexual relationship fit into your ideas about yourself, friendship, and what you want to do in the future?

The young man who thinks of himself as a "stud" and regards women as sexual objects often has deep-rooted insecurities about his maleness and expresses his fear of females by aggressive, punitive sexual behavior. The young man for whom sexual relations are an immediate necessity has probably not thought about the short-term effects of sexual activity, such as guilt or pregnancy, or the long-term effects of premature sex on his or his partner's life goals. Some men use sex to bolster their weak self-image and self-esteem; women may use sexual intercourse as a way to be liked and wanted. Intimate friendship rather than a sexual relationship may help you achieve success in school or athletics that would otherwise escape your grasp. People unable to make abiding friendships are unable to make abiding, satisfying sexual relationships; cool, angry people are not likely to be kind and gentle. In essence, friendship is the prerequisite for intimacy and intimacy is the prerequisite for sexual intercourse.

2. What about love?

Love is a state of existence that eludes easy definition. It is usually easiest to judge its existence and quality by the manifestations of love: affection, trust, abiding concern and mutual respect, consideration, humor, tenderness, and continuous growth as a person. Sexual intercourse in the absence of love is usually a convenience, often unfulfilling, and occasionally destructive. Loving behavior is characterized by honesty with yourself and others. Amoral or immoral sexual behavior is never associated with love.

3. What do you expect from sexual intercourse?

The overemphasis on sex in these times has created the myth that successful intercourse is easy. It isn't. While sex is indeed natural, it takes time, effort, and gentleness to learn how to love and how to make love. The young man who is unaware of this is usually ignorant or selfishly motivated. He is the perpetrator of dreadful first sexual experiences and often impedes his own and his partner's sexual spontaneity and growth.

4. Is sexual intercourse necessary for the relationship?

Sexual intercourse by itself is not enough to sustain an intimate, growing relationship. Adolescents who regard intercourse as a necessity use sex as a substitute for intimacy and love. Sexual intercourse should be a choice, not a necessity! No one should ever feel forced to have sexual intercourse. One always has the right to say no. In legal language, forced intercourse is known as rape.

5. If you plan to have a sexual relationship, what will you do if you need help?

As discussed before, many young people who never consider the possibility of personal or mutual distress also never consider where or whom to go to for help. Although information on contraception, conception, abortion by informed, sympathetic people is readily available, some adolescents do not know how to make use of these counseling services. You may be afraid or embarrassed to ask: you may not trust the Establishment. If you are too afraid or embarrassed to ask, imagine what the fear of pregnancy or unsuccessful sex would do to you. What will you do if you catch VD? What will you do if you start a pregnancy?

6. Have you thought about how the relationship might end?

It is relatively easy to have sexual intercourse once, but it is a major commitment to make a loving relationship which includes continuing sexual activity. Conversely, it is difficult to have continuing sex without a major commitment. It is a myth to think that sex on a trial basis is less of a commitment than marriage and therefore less upsetting when the relationship ends. Rejection is rejection whether we call it puppy love, trial marriage, or adolescent turmoil. Will it end with the bitterness of unwanted pregnancy, with the righteous indignation of a lover spurned, or will it quietly expire in the depressing realization that truly romantic and erotic sexual activity is the exception and not the rule? These questions are only a guide. Hopefully, they will help you to think about sex in perspective, with all of its ramifications, as an important, but not all-encompassing aspect of living and growing. Responsibility in sexual matters, as in other areas of life, is essential to respect: respect for yourself, respect for others, respect for the precious and fragile state known as life.

MORE READINGS ABOUT SEX

American Friends Service Committee. *Who Shall Live? Man's Control Over Birth and Death.* New York: Hill and Wang, 1970. A thoughtful presentation of the ethical problems of contraception, abortion, and death.

Boston Women's Health Collective. *Our Bodies, Ourselves.* New York: Simon and Schuster, 1973. A book of information and feelings about women's bodies by women.

Hettlinger, R. F. *Sex Isn't That Simple: The New Sexuality on Campus.* New York: Seabury Press, 1974. A sympathetic study of the sexual scene of college students. Careful attention to facts and feelings of students.

Liberman, E. J., and Peck, E. *Sex and Birth Control: A Guide for the Young.* New York: Thomas Y. Crowell, 1973. Detailed book discussing contraception and sexual behavior in a practical, straightforward manner.

Sorenson, R. C. *Adolescent Sexuality in Contemporary America.* New York: World Publishing Co., 1973.

The Student Guide to Sex on Campus. New York: New American Library, 1971. An excellent review of facts and philosophy prepared by Yale University students with the leadership of Dr. Philip Sarrel. Straightforward and easy to read.

Whelan, S. T., and Whelan, E. M. *Making Sense Out of Sex: A New Look at Being a Man.* New York: McGraw-Hill, 1975. A good review of sex and sexuality for boys. A companion volume for girls has also been published.

RELATIONSHIP CHOICES

Choosing Friends

Male friendships aren't as easy to come by as they appear in the cowboy movies. Playing in sports, fighting in wars, and drinking together rarely produce deep and lasting friendships. You are often given the false idea that the truest form of friendship is male friendship. One reason that these friendships are so difficult is that people are all so busy that there is little time to show interest in others, and therefore little inclination to find out about each other's hopes, fears, problems, and dreams.

"Competition," rather than sharing problems and joys, writes Marc Feigen Fasteau in *The Male Machine,* "is the principal mode by which men relate to each other." "This competitiveness feeds the most basic obstacle to openness between men, the inability to admit to being vulnerable. Real men, you learn early, are not supposed to have doubts, hopes and ambitions which may not be realized. Such feelings and concerns are part of everyone's inner life, but a man is taught he must be quiet about them. Often men do not share even ordinary uncertainties and half-formulated plans of daily life with their friends. And when they do, they are careful to suggest that they already know how to proceed—that they are not really asking for help or understanding."

Cooperation (sharing) is the basic foundation of

44 *Harold N. Boris*

friendship. But you can't be in constant competition and cooperate. You can't put yourself in another's place (empathize) and see your friend from his point of view through competition. You can't be in competition with your friend and always be considerate, nor find humor in each other's competitiveness, nor trust one another. The development of competition in a young man's life denies him the basic qualities necessary for sharing: empathy, trust, consideration, and humor.

"The problem with cooperation for men," says Jack Nichols in *Men's Liberation*, is that "cooperation means some degree of yielding. Yielding is considered weakness. Weakness is presumed the trait of a sissy. A sissy is queer. Hence an iron fist is the best posture these men know!"

Men who live within the masculine mystique are taught that they must be independent rather than inter-dependent; they must be cool rather than to express their feelings; they must be in competition and dominating relationships rather than cooperative and sharing in their friendships. The devastating result is that many men live without meaningful and close friends. The young man who values friendship knows that other young men are more than guys to measure yourself against and to compete against just as he knows that young women are more than potential dates, lovers, and wives. Friends are more than people to play with, work with, or of some use to you; friends are people to *be* with.

Harold N. Boris, psychologist, writer, and an active parent of three children, writes about the art of friendship. He suggests ways for you to learn how to be a friend and how to have friends.

Choosing Friends

BY HAROLD N. BORIS

Some people make friends who are as much like them as possible, even down to the clothes they wear and how they walk and talk.

Tom hangs around with Dick and Harry. They are not members of a gang, but their scuffed white sneakers, blue jeans, and Levi's jackets are like a uniform. They wear their hair the same way, and when they walk a person can't help thinking of John Wayne. They also talk alike. They speak in a mostly scornful way, putting down other kids, teachers, schools, and adults. They greet each other by saying "Hey, man! How's it going?" and they use a semiprivate vocabulary based on rock words.

They like each other a lot, though they would feel ashamed to say so. They have the idea that affection only takes place between girls or maybe later, between a woman and a man.

But there is a good solid reason why they like each other so much. Each of them is not very sure of himself. If people disagree with them about something or if they disagree with others about something, they can really feel worried. Or, what's worse, they can feel depressed, which really means feeling bad and sad at the same time. Though you would never guess it from the way they talk, they care a lot about what people—their teachers, other kids, and their families—think of them.

A bad grade on a paper could, just like a harsh word from one or the other of their parents, send them spinning into worry and feelings of worthlessness.

But fortunately, having one another as friends gives Tom, Dick, and Harry, like the Three Musketeers, an all-for-one, one-for-all spirit. Like the early colonists, by hanging together they avoid "hanging" separately. Their policy of mutual reinforcement not only protects them against external "enemies"—people who might insult or put them down in some way—it protects them against criticism from inside themselves—self-doubt, insecurity, feelings of inferiority, and the like.

It feels awful, of course, to go anyplace—school, downtown, or to a party—where people might think you are a nothing. It helps tremendously to have a friend not only at your side, but on your side. In fact when people meet for the first time, they ordinarily go about finding things in common in order to develop just such an on-one's-side relationship as soon as they can. There was recently an interesting experiment on this subject. A teacher drew several lines two feet long on the blackboard. They were all equal in length except one, which was an inch or two smaller. Most of the class was asked to say that *all* the lines were the same size, but certain students had been taken out of the room and didn't hear this plan. Then one by one they were brought back to the room to look at the lines. Each noticed that one line was shorter, but each changed his or her mind when he or she discovered that the rest of the class disagreed. It is hard to be the "only" one.

This experiment illustrates a friendship that enables each to feel that the best part of the world—his other two friends—are just like him. And each feels support and encouragement from the others. But to get this help, they have to be good friends back. None of them can feel free to disagree. If the other two said the lines were equal, the third one would have to believe it—*even when he knew it wasn't true.* They have to be *for* the same things, and *against* the same things so that they will be as much alike as possible.

Most friends have things in common. This is often what people say about their friendships: "I like so-and-so because we have a lot in common." But how much in common? Some of the best friendships are good exactly because of the differences between people. But differences, as we have seen, can be unsettling—leading to arguments or even fights. There are differences that are good and exciting ones, as when someone knows how to do something and you don't, but he's willing to teach you. All differences can be what enriches a friendship if the people involved learn how to *enjoy* them.

For example, there are arguments that help us to learn and there are arguments that are destructive. Helpful arguments stimulate each person to think, feel, and grow, and ultimately to grow close. In fact, there is probably no real friendship, marriage included, which hasn't become better as a result of a fierce dispute. However, a person who fails to express his deep-down emotions and thoughts will have only superficial and tentative relationships. Though he is seldom alone, more often than not he will feel lonely.

The ability to be yourself while letting the other person be him- or herself, despite the differences in viewpoint, custom, style, and conviction, has to develop in a friendship or the friendship never develops.

But it's hard to reveal yourself to people who, even though they are acquaintances, feel like strangers. Will they like me? What will they think? What will they do? Can they be trusted? These are tough questions, and they can't really be answered for sure unless and until you take a chance. Most talk is designed more to conceal than to reveal. But it is not until you take the risk of revealing yourself that you know whether there is a friend there in that other person or not. That is one facet of friendship. Another is to be a person in whom others can confide. You do not have to say "Me, too" to establish common likes, dislikes, or experiences. You can say, "That's about a million miles from where I'm at," and discover how fascinating it is to hear how the other person feels.

People who are curious about others have a greater variety of friends, which are not confined to boys with boys, girls with girls, jocks with jocks, intellectuals with intellectuals. Boys and girls can be good friends without going together, and people interested in cars can be friends with people interested in chess. Nor is it essential to have friends in the same age bracket. Older people and younger have developed substantial friendships. While they may disagree about all sorts of things, from sex to politics, the disagreements can widen each other's world as each person struggles to make himself or herself known.

When you allow yourself to experience differences in people, you may risk an increase in self-doubt, insecurity, and self-consciousness which may make you feel uneasy. But you don't have to *be* like the other person any more than he or she has to change to be more like you. Another risk may be dissimilar interests which present conflicts in how you spend your time. For example, you may want to work on an engine while your friend wants to play ball. Occasional sharing of each other's interest will strengthen your friendship yet allow you time for yourself.

All living things interact and are interdependent. So it is with the perfect friendship. The perfect friendship may be a series of friendships taken together: a friendship of Tom with Harry but also Tom with Manuel and Tom with Maria and Tom with Juan's grandfather and Tom with Bailey's kid brother and Tom with his mother and Tom with his geometry teacher, who bores him in class but fascinates him with his jazz collection.

Friendship has also been called an art. The art of it, however, does not begin with others, but with yourself. Friends who care for you help you to care for yourself through respect and acceptance. But to depend on others to do this for you usually means that you won't take risks. As a child you depended on the love and opinions of your parents. Then, anywhere from six years old on up you begin to turn to your friends. This freed you from being a papa's boy or a mama's boy and helped you to be yourself. However, it is also possible for people like Tom to go from dependence on parents directly into dependence on friends. Only the people have changed. The dependence hasn't.

Since the art of friendship comes first from learning how to be alone with yourself, to stand loneliness without feeling useless, worthless, afraid, or too sad, you are now freer to choose your friends. You can say "yes" and you can say "no." You can be yourself. Being able to be yourself means you allow other people to be themselves, and indeed are interested in their being so. You can be dependent and independent at the same time. Sometimes you can lean and sometimes you can be supportive. Sometimes you will seek encouragement and sometimes you will give it. This exchange is called interdependence. And interdependence takes time. Usually you get together around something—a game, an activity, an event. Gradually you learn to enjoy being with people with whom you feel safe because they like you and are like you. Later you may seek people who are different from you but who like you. Finally you can come to like people who are different from you and who don't yet like you. But this is the toughest of all: to learn to like someone who doesn't think you are all that great.

Happiness is one of the rewards of friendship. Happiness comes when we have learned to choose without being too choosy, to join in without losing our individuality, to take strength from commonality but to cherish differences. In short, to enjoy a range of people without trying to become exactly like them or to convert them into becoming exactly like us.

Marriage and Communications

Something happens to lovers when they marry. Suddenly they go from "me" and "you" and what interests me or you, our abilities, and what motivates us, to "husband" or "wife" and what role a man or woman has to play when they are married.

The traditional idea of marriage, where a man will be the lifelong economic support system for the woman —the great provider—in exchange for the domestic, child-raising, and social services of a wife who frees him to be out making the money, is found to be completely unhealthy.

Marc Fasteau, author of *The Male Machine*, writes that, "In the traditional marriage, the wife's world shrinks with the passage of time to house and children, and with it her self-confidence and sense of being in touch with the outside world. The self-description 'I'm just a housewife,' whether delivered defiantly or shamefully, sums up how many women feel about that status."

The jokes that men make about "getting caught," "getting trapped," or "tied down" when they marry is contrary to the evidence that married men thrive— they are on the top of the list in terms of mental health compared to married women, or single men or single women. Married women do just the opposite—their adaptation to a traditional marriage results in depression and passivity. A married woman has three times the number of severe neurotic symptoms that her single sisters have!

Warren Farrell, author of *The Liberated Man*, has described how the male-female division of labor within a relationship leads to a division of interests and closes communications between partners. Dr. Farrell stresses that as long as the breadwinning role is defined as the male role, men will measure themselves as a real man only by the amount of money they make.

It's not marriage that has to go—because all living arrangements have the same communications problems, as Dr. Farrell points out. It's the traditional role where each partner's behavior is determined only by his or her sex that stifles people in marriage. A marriage where the husband has all the stress and responsibility for making money and the woman has to live within his control and decisions because he makes the money is impossible for both the man and woman. Our culture values making money more than raising children and keeping house, which gives the male more prestige; but he pays for his cultural support with his life. Ulcers, heart attacks, and a shortened life span are often the price men have to pay for total responsibility.

An alternative to the traditional roles of husband and wife is an equal partnership marriage or relationship which assumes each person does what he or she does best rather than what each does because they are male or female.

Equal partners mean you are both in on deciding what each of you will do. Cooking, making money, raising children, painting the house, cutting the grass, and doing the laundry are all necessary for the partnership to function. Equal partnership doesn't mean you both have to paint the house or raise the children; it does mean you will decide who will do what on the basis of who is best at it, or who has the most time and interest in the job, or who hates it the least, instead of deciding on the basis of being male or female. Equal partners doesn't mean you are both the same, or even that you could be the same. It means you both have equal opportunity and equal responsibility to raise children and food, to make money and decisions.

When you understand an equal partnership, you won't be tied to the measurement of a man that says he is best because he makes the most money. Both of you in the partnership will have time and energy to have interests and friends and meaningful work. Equal partnership relationships are best for each member of the partnership. It's the only loving environment possible for survival.

Marriage and Communications

BY WARREN FARRELL

Dinner was over. After leaving the room I walked back toward our guests, my brisk pace unconsciously giving away, "Certainly, my company could not amuse themselves without my presence." From the archway of the living room I looked up and found, to my mixed emotions, everyone involved in conversation. Two groups. The women in the kitchen. The men around the coffee table. "C'mon, the Yankees will never be like they used to—once CBS bought them it was all over . . ." Guess which conversation?

"Anyone want a Michelob?" I asked, with my eye contact on the men.

It was only our third year of marriage, and I was self-consciously pleased I could offer a Michelob—it was just a bit more expensive than the Bud, Schlitz, Miller's variety, and, even though I was a student and my partner* was earning all the income, I still felt like more of a man offering the Michelob.

---

* Partner—A person with whom one shares a deep emotional relationship, although not necessarily sexual. It can be a woman, man, or both, and used instead of boyfriend, girlfriend, wife, husband and/or lover. It can be the person or persons one lives with in a marriage, extended family, or commune, or a person with whom one does not live—as long as the deep emotional relationship exists. Adapted from *The Liberated Man* (New York: Bantam, 1975).

"Yeah, could use a beer . . . got a Heineken cold?"

"Let's see." (I feel put down, open refrigerator, appear to be checking, knowing I never bought any.)

"Sorry, guess we're out."

I grab a Michelob from the refrigerator, turn around to my partner, and her women friends' conversation, and lean over to kiss my partner, while passing through to the men in the living room. A woman quickly makes space for me in the circle and another asks, "Warren, what do you think is best—having the boy be the oldest child, or the girl?" As a student of political science at the time I didn't have the foggiest, but quickly responded, "Oh, the boy—then they can each date each other's friends."

"See, I told you so," one of the women beamed.

My partner and I exchanged glances—my glance just a bit more self-confident than before, hers just a bit more approving.

A few minutes later we were engaged in a dispute about the politics of the Vietnam War.

"The problem is getting in there halfway and . . ."

"Bullshit . . . the problem is getting in there to begin with—it was all an economically based motive. In the capitalist system, new markets . . ."

"New markets, hell . . . it was the tungsten and rubber that . . ."

"C'mon, if we had bombed Hanoi at the outset, then . . ."

No one was hearing out anyone's point. None of us was drawing out anyone to find out more of the reasons his thinking developed to the point it did. But most interestingly, Ursie, my partner, had been standing behind me this whole time and neither I nor any of the other men had parted to let her in the circle, nor asked her a serious question about her opinion as I had been asked about boy children. Finally, her presence was recognized.

"Hi, Ursie—hey, that was a super meal you cooked today . . ."

"Yeah, no wonder Warren's getting a tummy . . ." (laughter—from everyone but me).

"Looking good . . . I like your dress" (one of the men's hands falls on Ursie's shoulder, touching the dress material, and slowly withdraws).

Ursie asks me a quick factual question just about whisper level, I respond, she smiles acknowledgingly at the "compliments," and returns to the kitchen.

The scene was repeated perhaps a hundred times in one form or another during the first four years of our marriage. It may be worth examining for its implications as to what happens to marriage, why about a third end up in divorce despite the fact that millions of couples stay together only for the children, or for the image, or because neither has the courage to divorce. In other words, while two-thirds may not end in divorce, many men and women admit, in the privacy of a confidential group, that they should. Let's glance back at the dinner scene and pick up some of the reasons.

One could walk into the apartment of our dinner party and physically see the gap between the men and the women. When we got married or first lived together, we were students and had our own independent lives, we talked together more or less as equals and shared common interests. After we were married, we conversed more or less as a wife or husband is expected to communicate. Now, the men had already begun to get involved in business or advanced academic work. We were involved in the world outside of the home and were talking about that world. If our area of occupations were too far apart, we'd weld it together by discussing sports or politics. Yet the women, in their own corner, were talking mostly about the world related to the home—children, recipes, decorating, possible new places to move, and, occasionally, what we, their partners, were doing. Even though some of our partners were working in the business or academic world, they perceived the *essence* of their future as the home. We perceived our essence as our work. *Our division of labor had led to a division of interests.* The gap between the men and women in the apartment was only symbolic of the gap between us in our lives.

Either consciously or unconsciously, many couples

recognize that something seems less fulfilled than it was. Then a cycle begins when something seems unfulfilled in a male-female relationship and the conclusion is often that the problem is the woman's. For an unfulfilled woman the "solution" is often a child. Sure enough, the child's problems take the focus off the couple's problems, and the couple sticks together focusing on the child or children until they grow old enough to leave home for work, college, or marriage. Then the couple is left with a vacuum. They look at themselves again—usually after about twenty-five years of marriage. Now they usually admit the gap between them. The divorce rate soars, the psychologists benefit, lawyers profit, and the couple either works to put Band-Aids on the gap, ignores it, separates, or lives under the guise of a happy marriage while transferring their passion for each other into work, volunteer activity, or someone else. In most cases, the fundamental problems are not overcome, and in many cases, the couple divorces, remarries, and brings at least the communication problems of sex roles for husband and wife into the new marriage.

Married people have three central things working against them: (a) the institution of marriage, (b) the sex roles they play that divide labor and interests, and (c) communication problems. Younger persons often focus on structural problems ("the problem is marriage as an institution—especially in a capitalist society") and ignore communication and sex role problems. Middle-aged and older persons often ignore all three areas, and only a small percentage of younger persons focus on sex role problems.

The importance of understanding sex role and communication problems is that they exist in fairly similar form in almost any structure of living together. They exist in monogamous marriage, closed marriage, open marriage, group marriage, communal, living together, celibate, or asexual living arrangements, or most combinations of these.

A closer look at the dinner party scene will reveal

just a few of many examples of these communication and sex role problems, most of which could exist in *any structure of living together.*

The one-upmanship about the Michelob and Heineken beer appeared to be a type of male bonding, or commonality of interest. It does serve the purpose of creating a dialogue that effectively excludes women, but it also is one more barrier to men communicating openly and personally with each other. In fact, conversely, it creates unspoken insecurities ("I don't earn enough to afford a Heineken") and anxieties ("Hopefully, I'll get that next promotion, then I can afford this type of thing"). In the atmosphere of one-upmanship, it seems gauche to say, "I feel bad about not being able to afford the type of beer you prefer," or for the man asking for the Heineken to respond, "You know, I really can't tell that much difference among the beers, but I feel more secure asking for one with a status label."

Each of the men at the dinner party, myself in particular as the host, was manipulated by the millions of messages coming through to men every day which suggest we should surround ourselves with symbols of success. Look at most ads for Scotches, cigarettes, stereo systems, or sports cars. Old Grand-Dad Bourbon puts it succinctly: "If not for yourself, for your image." Johnnie Walker Black Label's every ad manipulates men as success objects. One example of the only writing on a full-page ad:

Twinkle, twinkle superstar
To those who said you wouldn't go far
You showed them guts, you showed them nerve
Now show them by the scotch you serve

How does this manipulation of men as success objects hurt a marriage? On the simpler level it diverts men from talking about more human, less success-oriented things which would give our conversation, and therefore our interests, more overlap with women. It perpetuates the division of interests. Secondly, it makes us feel possessive about our success as if it were related to our masculinity, wanting therefore to keep out any woman who might enter our domain for fear she might threaten our masculinity. This was symbolized by our unconsciously keeping Ursie, my partner, out of our circle while we were talking politics. In addition to diverting ourselves from discussing human concerns on a personal level, this also discourages women from developing interests on a more success- or career-oriented level.

Thirdly, the manipulation of men as success objects tends to make us compete for supremacy, not only among women, but also in particular among men, not only during our participation in work, but also during our participation in almost any conversation. For example, as we discussed the Vietnam War, we competed with each other to make the point. We did not listen. We *self-listened*. That is, we listened for just long enough (usually a few seconds) to pick up the gist of what another person was saying, then started forming in our own mind's eye a story related to our own ego, background, or prior information. As soon as it is formed, we start nodding our head, waiting for a pause, and, with the briefest of pauses, jump in with our own contribution. We've usually missed most of the subtle points made by the other person, and even if we've heard the points well enough to repeat them if immediately challenged, we haven't really *considered* them because we've been forming our own interpretations.

Self-listening is central to miscommunications in most relationships—no matter what the structure. Men self-listen to other men, and women self-listen to other women. But when men and women get together and are discussing something of *serious* concern to them both, my own research has uncovered that men self-listen to women much more than women self-listen to men. In fact, women often *pseudo-listen*, an example of which was also apparent at the dinner party. When I was asked how I felt about a boy being older than the girl,

I contributed a response already known to the group. There was less reason to believe that my background at the time—a childless political scientist—would have contributed as much as one of the women with children, one of whom had an M.A. in child psychology and another of whom taught school. Yet I was not only asked, but my response, although already suggested by a woman in the group, became the basis for another woman feeling validated in her response (she beamed, "See, I told you so").

Pseudo-listening, then, is a process of asking a question to which one already knows the answer to make the other person look good, rather than really needing to know the answer. Pseudo-listening might also be used as a source of unneeded validation by a person who places too much weight in an authority figure, but it is frequently used by women with the knowledge of what they are doing—building a man's false ego. The problem with it is that while the woman learns little, the man develops a fragile foundation that then requires still more women to support or prop it up.

These are some of the simpler levels on which men being manipulated as success objects hurts a marriage or relationship. On a more fundamental level, *as long as the breadwinning role is defined as the male role, men will think of themselves as more of a man the higher they climb in that role.* Accordingly, they will induce anxieties, peptic ulcers, heart attacks and commit suicides and acts of violence at much higher rate than women to fulfill that role. They will try to keep women out of that role to retain its identity as an all-male role.

In the process, many men cut out an area of specialization and hold onto it for life, even after it has become repetitious and boring. Even after they have stopped growing, stopped the creative questioning that marked them as young men, and have begun to find themselves justifying last year's budget, worrying about increasing the size of their staff to give themselves the appearance of more power, becoming, in essence, a bureaucrat. If they are blue-collar workers, they often set on making sure their wife doesn't work, and if she does, their goal is often to be able to provide the income "without her help," to prove themselves an adequate breadwinner (translation: an adequate man). Neither sees the freedom evolving to men whose partner shares the responsibility for earning the income—freedom to switch jobs, be underemployed or unemployed for a while while training for a more interesting area that may pay less, but be more meaningful work to the man. When a man can switch jobs without fear of leading his family into the poorhouse, he obtains the freedom to question and remain creative on whatever job he takes. What struck me during my work with consciousness-raising or awareness groups for men all over America and Canada is how many high-school and college men agree to this in theory, but say, "Oh, I'll be different." When I meet them three or four years after graduation, they're saying, "Well, I can't question that point now," or "I can't change jobs now." "I have a wife and family to support—I'll have to wait just a few more years, until I get in a position where I can really change things." "Just a few more years."

When the women's liberation movement came along, an alternative was presented. Many women suggested they might want to share the responsibility for earning the income if the men shared the responsibility for child care and housework. On the one hand men were watching TV commercials of the independent, pioneering spirit of the Marlboro man, responsible in his aloofness to none. In their personal lives, though, they were only living out this image vicariously or indirectly, by smoking a Marlboro or watching a football game. When presented with the opportunity for women to share the load of breadwinning, they only looked at the threat, not at the *potential* for using that security base of another income to pioneer in some undeveloped terrain of their life. Few considered returning to school, learning a new trade, working part-time, learning to love their children. Many used the escape mechanism, "Well, my wife couldn't earn as much as I do." Few understood that they wouldn't be earning as much themselves if their partner had not been willing to move with them occasionally for a better job opportunity, or listen to them supportively when they came home from work, or to take full responsibility for their children, or do most of the housework.

Some men were not threatened by their partner playing superwoman—being involved in a career, child care, and housework full time—they just got threatened when they had to do some of the domestic work themselves or any time was taken away from them. And this will always appear a threat as long as men block themselves from pursuing many different interests during a lifetime for fear they will not go as high up the ladder or earn as much income as they can. This division of labor will lead to divisiveness in any relationship, whether it be two lovers turned living friends, or a husband and wife. Whatever the structure of the relationship or life-style, the communication problems perpetuated by narrow images of men's and women's roles are central.

The women's movement, working together with men's liberation, has introduced a chance for equal partnership to be more than rhetoric. One option toward that equality is sharing financial responsibility, freeing the man to have interests other than making money, and sharing child care and housework, freeing the woman to have interests other than being mother and homemaker. Both can enjoy the external rewards of success without being trapped into a specialization. Both can enjoy the human rewards of parenting without being so involved with the children we need to control them or live our own lives through them. Equal partnership provides an environment that is best for each person in the family.

LIBERATION CHOICES

The Liberated
Young Man

On first thought, women's liberation seems to be against men—to put men down in order to gain equality for women. Women's liberation appears to take away from men.

But for those of you who take a closer look—the purpose of women's liberation is *not* for a woman to be more like a man and take his sports, his jobs, his college graduate school places, and his total control over relationships. The purpose of liberation for both men and women is for both of them to become more human. More a unique person rather than a stereotype (generalizing that all girls and all boys have certain behavior and role characteristics).

Warren Farrell, author of *The Liberated Man* and founder of over two hundred men's consciousness-raising groups and the first national conference on the Masculine Mystique, begins this chapter with a role-reversal date. That is, the men played the "boys" who were asked out on a date and they passively acted as people usually do when being dated. Young women played the person who initiates a date and they had control over what the couple was going to do. Dr. Farrell wants you to feel what it's like to be on the other side of dating. Not that you are to act like a woman—but rather to act like a person who is asked out and has no active control over how the relationship and date will go, as women are trained to act. The effects of liberation on the issues of dating, sports, and a woman's negative image are described in this chapter.

What's in liberation for you? As women are liberated from their stereotype of being passive, emotional, and completely dependent upon men, men will become free to be more who they are meant to be. Free to choose to be independent and sometimes dependent; active sometimes and passive sometimes; cool sometimes but expressing their feelings at other times. Controlling some relationships and not others— controlling at times in one relationship and their partner in control at other times. What's in it for you is that it's the first time a group is encouraging you to say—"wait a minute— that's not me—I'm not like all males—I'm not a male stereotype. I'm a real man and and it's like this . . ." Notice what kind of a guy you are. Trust your own experience of you and be free to choose . . . to be fully human.

The Liberated Young Man

BY WARREN FARRELL

It's Saturday night. Six o'clock. No one's asked me out yet. The basement is cold. Looking gloomier each minute. Waiting . . . waiting to be asked. I look up at the woman gathered near the wall across from me in the basement. They're standing confidently, looking assured. I'm too nervous to notice their nervousness. I feel the other men's presence, feel their awkward stances as the women look us over—feeling like . . . well, like meat on a rack.

The scene is a role-reversal date at Georgetown University. It's part of a consciousness-raising weekend held each semester to raise the awareness of the way sex roles hurt both sexes. I've been coordinating the weekend. Until now I have never been evaluated solely by how I look or by how I come off physically. I'm worrying, Are my shoulders straight, is my stomach tucked in? I remember that survey in some magazine that women like flat stomachs. And nice rears. I've gone from success object to sex object.

Nervously, I count the number of women on the opposite wall. I feel a sigh of relief. There are two more women than men. Somebody will have to ask me out, I reassure myself. I can barely believe this "role-reversal date" was my idea.

"Why don't you men turn around so we can get a rear view?" one of the women shouts. Their instructions

were to look us "boys" over as sex objects. I tuck my
rear in. And turn. Is it O.K.? I try to pick up a reflec-
tion of myself in the glass on the door. We "boys" are
supposed to look the women over as "success objects":
"What type of car you going to take me out in?" one
of the "boys" asked coyly. "Oh, a seventy-seven
Porsche," returns an assured voice.

"Warren, can't we ask the boys out yet? I can't take
this any longer, and I'm getting butterflies," laughs
Maria nervously.

"You're out of role, Miss—er, Ms.," one of the boys
objects. "If you were a man, you wouldn't be able to
admit you were nervous."

"*You're* out of role. If you were a woman you'd
know your place and keep your mouth shut!"

"And besides, I'm not Ms., I'm Dr."

We all laugh. But I remember the pressure I exerted
on myself for years to have that "Dr." in front of my
name.

Some of the women gather together in groups. "What
a piece of . . ." one remarks. She's not looking at me.
I'm not sure whether I'm glad or mad.

"His hairline looks like the latest recession," con-
tributes another woman, pointing to the older "boy"
next to me.

"What a spare tire that boy has. . . ."

"Maybe he's pregnant!"

"C'mon, who would want to get *him* pregnant?"

"Let's see your hand size boys—there's an old
wives' tale . . . I mean an old husbands' tale . . . that
says a boy's hand size is related to the size of his most
fragile instrument."

"Most fragile instrument?"

"No, not your egos—the other one!"

Everyone laughs again. But we're all glancing awk-
wardly at our hand size. Which was O.K., because it
was the first time I knew what to do with my hands.
Being looked over like this was having a devastating
impact on my body language.

I almost forgot. I'm supposed to be conducting this

weekend. I ask the women to come forward, pick their "boys," and end this agony.

They meander toward us. But too slowly. I quickly think to myself which woman I would like to have ask me out. Oh, yes. The one with the straight hair and brown corduroys. Damn it! It doesn't make any difference whom *I* want. The women are deciding. I feel powerless. My eyes drop from an assertive, intense scanning to a seductive, passive sparkle.

Two women eventually wander toward me. But they stop to talk to each other. They cast sly glances my way. I use the only option I have—I decide which one I'm most interested in, and play coy. I wink.

She doesn't pick up the hint. The other woman comes over and asks me out. "Well, er, O.K., well, what type of career do you have?"

"I'm in law school."

"Freshman?"

"No."

"What, then?"

"Freshwoman."

"Oh," (Pause.) "What type of law are you going into?"

"Well, I'm going to take over the family business a few years after I graduate."

"Oh, I see. Your dad own a business?"

"No. My mom owns General Motors, and she'll be passing that on to me."

"Oh, I see." I forgot the women were allowed to exaggerate "a little."

"What are you doing?" she asked me.

"I'm going to teach kindergarten for a couple of years, and then I'd like to get married and take time off to raise our children."

"Oh, you're going to work before getting married, eh. Are you some type of boys' libber?"

"Oh, no. I'm no jockstrap burner. Do I look like that type of boy? But I do believe in equal pay **for equal** work."

"You're a cute little thing, you know that? How

about going out for a drink with me? There's a neat discotheque on the other side of town. C'mon along."

At the close of an interesting role-reversal night out she asks warmly, "You much into massage?"

Uh-oh, I think to myself, I know where this one's going—I'd better change the subject.

"Not much, but I'm really interested in all the traveling you've done—tell me about it." She's a bit taken aback, but recovers. "Well, one of my favorite places is Colorado—ever been there?"

"No . . ."

"You'd like it. Do you like John Denver?"

"Oh, yes."

"Really? Well I have some of Denver's best albums back at my place. I'm sort of a Denver freak. Why don't you come over and we can listen to them together?"

"Well, thanks, but I'm kinda tired and I have most of his albums . . . perhaps some other time," I offer, verbally exiting politely.

"You haven't heard them on a stereo system like mine," she comes back. "And if you're tired, you can relax on my water bed, and I'll give you a massage. You'll love it."

I can't believe it. It sounds great, but I remember our roles—she's supposed to try to go as far as she can with me, and then go back to all the other women and exaggerate how far she got. And me? I'm supposed to preserve my reputation. The problem is, I'm actually beginning to take this role seriously. I don't want her going back to the women bragging about everything the leader did!

"Thanks so much, but I really need to get back to my place and get a good night's sleep. All my books are there, and I have an exam first thing in the morning."

"Sunday?"

"Er . . . I mean first thing Monday morning." She takes me back to my place.

We discussed our role-reversal dates in detail when

we returned to the consciousness-raising group at Georgetown the next day.

As we examined the date, we picked out numerous dimensions which simultaneously hurt both sexes. Let's reconstruct the date from the beginning, examining its implications for less stereotyped male-female relationships. As I was waiting to be asked out, I felt powerless. I could understand how, if I had to do this over a lifetime, I would resent being unable to make plans ahead of time, how I could develop the dependency many men initially like because it makes them look good, but eventually find a burden. I was surprised to find myself becoming coy, indirect, and manipulative. Yet, in my normal male role I was forced always to have to risk rejection, to put on false airs of assuredness (driving speed, drinking the right liquor, tone of voice) while inside my heart was running amuck. While we think we're in control, we become so concerned with maintaining those airs we become insensitive to the ways we're being manipulated indirectly. In my role play as a woman I could feel myself developing a passive, introverted body language; as I was being looked over like meat on a rack I became more bodily self-conscious than I can ever remember. I could see the women, though, lose their warmth and sincerity I wanted to see men develop and, like many men, they took on a false relaxedness, an assertive stance, and a cocksureness.

I could hear the women start defining themselves through their status (Porsche, law profession, family business) in the same way I had, in my real life. I felt I would not be successful as a man until I received my Ph.D. I could feel the way I, playing the woman's role, began to repress my sexuality and feel guilty about what I didn't repress, the way I saw my date start to use manipulative devices, lies, exaggeration, big tips, and deception to obtain the sexuality I was repressing. She was forcing herself into acting the way she was expected to act.

A key to understanding sex roles is realizing that

the pressure on one sex to be one way pressures the other sex to be another way. These pressures polarize male and female. Both sexes lose by the pressure to conform.

LIBERATION AND DATING

While many persons in high school or college don't consider themselves as "dating" in the old sense of the word (they "hang out" together), and while few play out roles in as stereotyped ways as the manner in which we caricatured them during our reversal date, women and men still play out many of these roles in more subtle forms. Even among liberated women who have been trying to work out "liberated" relationships for years, few can recall even once initiating holding a man's hand, or kissing a man with feeling *before* he had ever taken any of those steps with her, or before the vibrations between them were *very* clear. In other words, the man was almost always expected to put his ego on the line, and the more he did it, the more fragile it became. Most women sense the fragility, and play the role of ego protector—never being too obvious about it. Women end up, as the saying goes, "always supporting, but never showing." In the end, women become hostile to the fragile male ego they've helped create, mocking it privately while protecting it publicly.

Both the women and man suffer from the fragile male ego and the anxiety and insecurity resulting when unliberated women put the burden on men by not sharing the risk of rejection. The more men accept this role of masculinity, as studies by Dr. Susan M. Gray indicate, the more likely they are to experience anxiety.

The anxiety and long-term insecurity men experience as a result of initiating friendships became apparent to me during my own research. I asked a random sample of hundreds of men from different socioeconomic classes to answer the following question "true" or "false": "I think I develop sexual relationships with women faster than most men." Social psychologists warned me that more than 90 percent would respond "true," since most men wanted to think of themselves as "real men." However, only 17.6 percent responded "true"; the remaining 82.4 percent responded "false."

When it is the male role to assume initiative, men are tempted to brag about how successful they are as a way of proving their manhood.

Most men exaggerate, some fabricate, and almost all relate only their more successful "conquests." Each man knows he is exaggerating, and he thinks the other men are, but he is never quite certain. As a result he develops a feeling of inadequacy, thinking the other men are more successful as men. As long as it is the male role to assume the initiative, we will need to exaggerate our success. We treat women as sex objects so as not to risk emotional involvement which may result in rejection of ourselves, and we become insecure at the gap between our own relationships with young women and the exaggerations of others. Both sexes lose.

Dating and sex are an area in which men can benefit from liberation. Men often complain that women's liberation puts them down. As we change our attitudes about young women and about sex, responding to women's assertiveness and their interest in good relationships, some of us are surprised to find ourselves even more interested in women. However, others of us still find ourselves worrying a lot about sex. Al, a student in an Ohio group, finally opened up with an explanation with which many men could identify: "My partner and I decided we didn't really want to get into sex with each other at this time in our lives but we did enjoy being touched, caressed, cuddled, and general closeness. Now we have started to put our focus on being close, on *sensuality*. We've gotten to like it so much that we aren't always in a hassle anymore about whether to have sex or not. We don't."

Another guy in the group said, "I've often done that type of thing—the sensuality stuff—before I've made love." Another man said, "That's what foreplay is all about."

"No," Jim came back, "foreplay is only *using* sensuality as preparation for the big play—it's not sensuality for its own sake. As long as you know you're using the sensuality, then there is still pressure to perform for the big act."

Men are often able to understand this concept in theory, but we haven't had the training to understand our own sensuality in the same subtle dimensions as musicians train themselves to be attuned to all the fine strains of music. Sensuality training courses are now being developed as an issue within the men's liberation movement. For example, sensuality feeding can be done, say, by slowly peeling an orange under someone's nose whose eyes are closed, touching the orange skin against a cheek, arm, or leg, parting a section of the orange and very slowly rubbing it first against your partner's lips, then teeth, and finally slowly feeding the orange to him or her. The partner usually picks up a whole new experience of touch, smell, and taste which tunes him or her into the many dimensions of sensuality, which is often missing in sex. Much of the sensuality men are training for is what women often experience. Women have and give a dimension of emotional and sensual involvement with which most men are not in touch.

IMAGE OF WOMEN AS A MEN'S ISSUE

Women's liberation is incorrectly seen as relevant only to women. For example, the media image of women is generally seen only as a women's issue. Children's books with stories saying "when you mix the clay [to make a woman], mix in guile and cunning, a shameless mind, a deceitful nature" seem to indicate only that the image of women is negative. However, *it is just this negative image of women that makes us as men afraid to do anything to develop the feminine parts*

*of our personality—for fear we will also be saddled
with this negative image.* Yet it is only by integrating
the best of the feminine and masculine parts of our
personality that we develop a human personality. The
negative image of women makes men afraid to compete equally with women, because they know that if
they win they gain no one's admiration, and if they
lose, it's to a woman who isn't even considered real
competition.

This fear of appearing like a woman also takes its
toll in schoolwork and a young man's intellectual
achievement. Boys become afraid of appearing to study
too hard "like a girl." If they do well in school, it should
just "come naturally." Many young men play cool with
schoolwork, academic creativity, and achievement for
fear it will not reinforce looking like a man. As a result,
young men lose out on these academic skills. *The one
common element among both high-achieving and highly
creative boys and girls is that neither adopts traditional
sex roles,* according to research on creativity by social
scientist E. P. Torrance.

The negative image of women also encourages
fathers to put pressure on boys not to do anything that
would appear feminine. Studies by sociologist E. W.
Goodenough show that fathers get more upset than
mothers when their children—especially boys—deviate
from "proper" sex role behavior.

Such fathers often discourage their sons from playing
a musical instrument or studying, while encouraging
him to "play ball like the other boys," or to "learn how
to fight so you can defend yourself." It can be in the
form of put-downs of hippies, flower children, the
"overeducated," or "weaklings" like welfare recipients.

LIBERATION AND SPORTS

In work with over two hundred men's groups in the
United States and Canada, I have encountered many
former football players, wrestlers, and weight lifters

who have, in retrospect, felt they put as much energy
as they did into the sports they played in order to prove
themselves worthy of their fathers' attention. As one
man explained, "During the week Dad used to come
home just a few hours before I went to bed. He was
tired and we didn't really communicate much until the
weekends. Then we'd sometimes do things together,
but it was usually playing ball, scouting, or something
like that. I guess I felt that if I wasn't good at those
things I wouldn't get my father's attention. Everyone
thought I was more secure because I got to be good at
those things. Actually I was less secure. I got to be good
at playing end in football, but I never had a chance to
develop my throwing arm or blocking ability. I was a
specialist—a sort of cog in a machine, used to produce
victories to entertain my family, friends, and others who
would be prouder of me. I guess I was bought. To say
nothing of the fact that I neglected sports I loved, like
tennis and swimming, and to say nothing of my studies
and my relationships with girls or a lot of other things
I neglected because I was so busy perfecting the thing
that gave me all the attention."

Another man picked up on this point with, "Yeah,
women always complain about being looked at as sex
objects. Well, I always felt like an 'athletic object.' I
mean, like every day I'd get out on the field, and if I
wasn't a captain choosing the sides, I'd have to stand
there and find out whether I was first, second, third, or
ninth chosen. It was like a daily masculinity report
card. I would have loved to have chosen one thing I
was good at, rule everything else out, perfect it, and
have people cheer me for that."

How does liberation affect men being used as athletic
objects? As one man expressed it, "In grammar school
I used to watch those cheerleaders doing somersaults
with their underwear showing for these guys playing
basketball in the gym. I thought to myself, If only I
could make it on the team—then I'd have an in with
them, too!" As women are increasingly encouraged to
play *on* teams when they want to, being "on the team"
will not be so exclusively a mark of manhood. Women

will not have to try to go out with the star athlete as a way of making themselves feel more feminine when star athletes are both men and women. And men, therefore, are less likely to feel "making it" on the team means "making it" with the right woman.

Cheerleaders appear to be supporters of men. In fact, *cheerleaders are also pressures*. They pressure men to perform, to be unhesitatingly self-confident, to not look inward or admit error. Men who try to keep women in that position end up putting that burden on themselves. The pressure to appear self-confident and unhesitating with women in dating, to have it appear "to just come naturally," is the same pressure that young men feel in sports.

Boys are often threatened when girls first get involved in sports, until they get to know them. Girls can share interests with boys, and sports become a way they can share time together (a difference between it being the *only* way they share time together, as is often the case among boys). It is self-defeating, then, for young men to feel threatened by something likely to enhance their relationship with young women with whom they may later also have a close relationship.

Many of the "super athlete" values of sports are being challenged. Part of our creative energies for co-educational sports needs to go into (a) the creation of cooperative ways of playing traditional sports, (b) the creation of new sports, and (c) the adoption of sports from other cultures that require cooperation as well as competition.

As long as we establish standards of what it takes to be a man, we'll be encouraging men to use sports as a way of proving themselves men rather than as a way of learning to work with each other regardless of who plays and who wins. Men's and women's liberation, then, like sports, can be seen not as another form of competition but as a way of sharing responsibilities so we have the freedom both to compete and to relax, to look inward and to discover ourselves. A liberated young man has the freedom to learn his *own* standards of what it takes to be a man.

TURNING-ON
CHOICES

Deciding About Drugs and Alcohol

Roger F. Aubrey, Director of Guidance and Health Education for the Boston suburb public schools of Brookline, works with, writes about, and is most concerned with high-school students in the present-day American drug culture.

Dr. Aubrey describes why young people drink and take drugs, how people are turned on and turned off from drugs, and how drugs affect your behavior. He writes that most people use mood-changing drugs for pleasure and fun. *No one* originally turns to drugs to increase their pain or to complicate their lives with more problems.

Deciding About Drugs and Alcohol

BY ROGER F. AUBREY

CASES OF DRUG TAKING BY YOUNG ADULTS

The first time Tom Sanders tried drugs was sixteen years ago. He was given his first injection by a doctor, and it probably saved his life. At that time, Tom Sanders was six months old and in a hospital with pneumonia.

The first time Charlie Hawk tried drugs was on his fifteenth birthday. On that day, he and twenty other American Indians were initiated into the rite of peyotism by his tribe in the Southwest. Part of the initiation ceremony included the drinking of a tea made from the peyote cactus plant. The usual results from taking this drug are hallucinations or distortions of the normal process of perception.

Bob Johnson has a hard time remembering his first drug experience. Bob is a heroin addict and has been on the street for years. His first memory of drugs goes back to early junior high school days. He used to skip school with friends and smoke marijuana and sip wine in friends' cars.

If alcohol is considered a drug (and it is, according to most medical experts), then Sam Pearlstein has been taking drugs most of his life. Sam's family usually has one or two glasses of table wine with dinner each evening. Since he was a small child, Sam and his brothers and sisters have joined their mother and father on these occasions.

David Temple takes a drug every day of his life. However, few people are aware of his need for this drug. He usually takes this drug before each meal; and if he doesn't, serious problems might occur. David suffers from a form of epilepsy and without this drug he might have seizures or convulsions.

With the exception of a few marijuana cigarettes, Bill Cunningham never entered his high school drug scene. However, at a graduation party, Bill was given a cube of LSD by one of his friends. Bill ended up in the emergency ward of a nearby hospital three hours later in a severe state of depression.

THE WIDE RANGE OF DRUGS

All of the young men just mentioned are alcohol or drug takers. Each on more than one occasion has swallowed, sniffed, smoked, or injected into his body a chemical substance changing the regular functioning of the brain and body. However, the main difference among these young men lies not in the fact that they take drugs or alcohol; rather, they differ because of the reasons behind their drug and alcohol taking and the specific drug or beverage selected to fulfill this purpose.

With the exception of small children, most individuals in the United States sample a wide variety of drugs and alcohol each year. In fact, we are encouraged to try many drugs and a variety of alcoholic beverages by advertisements on TV and radio, in newspapers and magazines, by advice from our friends, through the daily example of people around us, and by the easy availability of drugs and alcohol through legitimate and illegal sources.

The use of drugs in a broad sense includes all chemical substances taken into the body that cause changes in the physical and/or mental functioning of an individual. This broad definition therefore includes such common substances as coffee, tea, cigarettes, beer, wine, hard liquor, aspirin and other headache remedies, drugstore pills and liquids (not requiring a prescription) promising relief from pain or ease in sleeping, laxatives, birth control pills, and so on. All of these substances, and a great many more, can be classified as drugs because of their effect on our thinking processes or bodily functioning.

In a narrow sense, drug taking can be defined as the illegal or unlicensed use of a variety of drugs, including the use of alcoholic beverages by underaged adolescents. Some of the drugs in this category have a legitimate reason for being taken if they are prescribed by a medical doctor. Included here would be such drugs as tranquilizers (to relieve tension and anxiety), amphetamines (to stimulate or awaken), and barbiturates (to produce sleep or sedation). Also included in this category are drugs with no real medical use (heroin, airplane glue), or drugs used only for experimental purposes (LSD).

This chapter examines drug taking in its narrow sense. Our main focus is on drugs and alcoholic beverages that produce changes in the moods, emotions, and behavior of persons. Our concern is therefore restricted to a small number of drugs and narcotics. Alcohol is included because our definition of drugs includes alcohol. In fact, alcohol is the most frequently used and abused drug in the history of humankind.

ARE DRUGS GOOD OR BAD?

The word "drugs" means many things to many people. Most parents and law-enforcement officers feel "drugs" are bad, and there should be strict laws regulating their use. On the other hand, medical doctors would quickly say "drugs" are good and save thousands of people each year. Students, too, differ on how they view drugs. Some students feel drugs such as marijuana, like beer, should be legalized and available to everyone above a certain age: other students agree with law-enforcement officers on strict penalties for all persons illegally selling, buying, or using drugs.

Although most people have strong opinions about whether drugs and alcohol are good or bad, few individuals look beyond this question. Are drugs really bad? Is it wrong for someone in pain to have the pain eased by a drug? Is it wrong for a mature person to take a chemical substance to increase pleasure and satisfaction if this act does not harm anyone else? Finally, is it harmful for someone to experiment with drugs in order to gain valuable knowledge and information about himself?

The answers to these questions are not as simple as they might appear. Questions and answers go well beyond the simple problem of whether drugs and alcohol are good or bad. Instead of dealing with this endless debate, it seems much more useful to deal with the actual behavior of individuals using and not using drugs and alcohol. In this way we can avoid labeling drugs and alcohol good or bad, and instead discuss what occurs when a drug is abused or felt to enhance the behavior of a person.

Drugs, therefore, are not of themselves something wicked or evil. The problem with all drugs that are misused comes from the behavior of the person abusing the drug and not the drug itself. A man driving a car recklessly after drinking too much alcohol is exhibiting poor judgment both in regard to his driving and because he overindulged himself with alcohol. Persons who abuse drugs have allowed drug use to overwhelm and restrict the direction of their lives. In particular, individuals called "drug abusers" have developed specific patterns of drug use that weaken their growth as persons in social, vocational, career, spiritual, and personal areas.

WHO ARE THE DRUG AND ALCOHOL USERS?

Most people in the United States are drug and alcohol users in one form or another. Many of us begin using drugs when we first awaken in the morning. We may take an aspirin or pill for a headache and some people may take a vitamin or pep pill (amphetamine) to ensure a good day. Many more persons could not make it through the first hour without a cup of coffee or that first cigarette of the day.

As the day proceeds, many individuals will take a morning laxative or perhaps a painkiller to relieve a discomfort. Others will have a beer or cocktail with lunch, and some will smoke their first marijuana cigarette of the day. As lunch goes on, a great many people will pop a pill to aid their stomach in the digestion of food (or to deal with excessive gas and acidity). As night draws near, other patterns of drug usage appear. Some individuals literally live in a drug culture and use drugs throughout their every waking hour. They feel (and for some it may be true) they could not survive a full day without drugs.

Drugs are used and abused by millions of Americans. Recent estimates put the number of alcoholics in this country at approximately nine million. Add to this figure well over a half-million regular heroin users and the millions of Americans who could not function without their sleeping pills, diet pills, laxatives, alcohol, painkillers, and nicotine and you have just a slight idea of how many Americans use drugs and alcohol regularly.

Drug users and abusers are not always easy to distinguish. Someone dependent on a hundred-dollar-a-day heroin habit should be easy to spot. But an athlete who uses sleeping pills the night before key games, and pep pills before the game, may be harder to spot. For each, drugs have become a major part of their ongoing life-styles.

WHY USE DRUGS?

Study after study has shown there is no single pattern or easy explanation for why people become dependent on drugs and alcohol. For example, look at the list of reasons below for possible explanations of adolescent drug and alcohol taking. How many reasons could you add to this list?

Reasons for Adolescent Drug and Alcohol Taking

Alcoholic or drug-taking parents
Boredom with school and home
Parents too easy and permissive
Weakness of personality
Difficulty in getting along with others
Desire for new experience
Lack of love and affection
Search for a sense of meaning
Moral and spiritual confusion
Lack of goals and purpose
Influence of others
Inferiority feelings
Rebellion against parents
Loneliness
Curiosity/adventure
Escape from problems
Emotional immaturity
Enjoyment and pleasure
Pressure from school
Desire to act grown up

In looking over this list, you may have added a few more reasons. In fact, you yourself may have tried drugs or drinking for reasons other than on this list. Nevertheless, there are two reasons any drug taker would agree *are not* reasons for why he or she turned to drugs. First, no one turns to drugs to increase the amount of pain and frustration in their lives. Second, no one *originally* turns to drugs to increase the amount of problems in their lives.

A PARTIAL EXPLANATION FOR
DRUG AND ALCOHOL EXPERIMENTATION

The two reasons just mentioned are extremely important in understanding drug-taking behavior. Many people do take drugs and alcohol as a means of solving problems. These problems may range from shyness in meeting people to overweight to unhappiness and loneliness. For young men, the problem of "being one of the guys" and "a real man" often leads him to accept drinking as a means to adulthood and acceptance by the group. However, the list of problems leading to drug or alcohol experimentation is endless. The important fact is that drugs are seen by many people as a legitimate means of solving or relieving problems.

A second major reason for drug taking was overlooked for many years. Scientists, doctors, educators, and parents simply could not accept the fact that many people take drugs and alcohol because it gives them pleasure and satisfaction. Drugs for many people today are a means of social and recreational enjoyment. This fact is especially hard for parents and adults to accept, even though many of them have used alcohol for years for the same purpose. Today, these same parents have a difficult time in accepting the fact that most doctors and drug experts have placed alcohol in the same category as any other drug.

If we accept for a moment the simple explanation that people either take drugs partially to solve problems or to ease discomfort and increase pleasure, we have some chance of avoiding an argument. We also have a realistic way of examining the behavior of people who use drugs without making a judgment as to whether their behavior is bad or good. A man out of work, recently divorced, and in poor health should not be judged immoral or evil because he turns to alcohol to solve his problems and ease his pain. Even though this behavior may lead to more serious problems, judging another person's behavior is not a helpful way to understand his or her present life conditions.

The idea that individuals take drugs in order to gain pleasure and satisfaction is extremely difficult for many people to accept. However, these same people would probably agree that eating an apple pie or pizza at a party is quite all right. Dancing or listening to music are probably other activities these people would approve of at a social gathering. The list of activities pleasing to individuals could be endless, but the point is obvious: *different experiences produce pleasure in different individuals. And for many people today, drugs and alcohol are an acceptable and pleasing form of social and recreational entertainment.*

TURNING ON AND TURNING OFF

Turning on and using drugs and alcohol are very easy today. Turning off must be seen realistically as a more difficult process, unless we deny the existence of millions of people who lead a nightmarish life because of their complete dependency on drugs.

The term "drug or alcohol dependent" is used by doctors to describe people who cannot function in society without the use of these substances. Drug- or alcohol-dependent people require daily amounts of these chemicals just to survive both mentally and physically. Without drugs or alcohol, these people would have to be hospitalized or placed in treatment facilities.

On the other hand, "drug or alcohol dependent" describes a particular kind of person who is prone or susceptible to these chemical substances. Individuals who are so labeled may never in their lives have taken a drink or a drug. Nevertheless, their unique personality makeup is the type that could quite easily become dependent or reliant on drugs. These people, once they begin taking drugs, have an excellent chance of ending up "hooked," or addicted.

There are really two kinds of dependency on drugs.

One is that which comes directly from the drug itself, *physical dependency*. People in this category develop in their body system an actual physical need for the effects of a specific drug or alcohol. Without regular and daily amounts of the drug, pain and discomfort arise. Complete withdrawal or taking away of the drug or alcohol can in time cause extreme pain and suffering.

The other form of dependency is known as *psychological dependency*. In this case the person has come to rely on drugs as a means of dealing with life, people, and difficult situations. Instead of using inner strength and courage, the person has come to rely on drugs and alcohol to get through tough and demanding experiences. The effect of drugs has therefore weakened and lessened the ability of the person to deal with an inner source of strength. Instead a bottle or a pill must do the job.

The physical or psychologically dependent person has to be considered in any talk about drugs and alcohol because none of us wish to think of ourselves as potentially dependent. Those who never have taken drugs or alcohol can obviously say, "I've never done it so it can't happen to me." At the same time, those who have tried drugs on various occasions, with no ill effects, can also say, "No—not me—I can turn off anytime I want to." Finally, those really into drinking or drugs can say, "I can quit anytime I want. . . . Sure, I'm really into this thing now, but I wasn't always and I can really get clean anytime I want."

WHAT'S IN IT FOR YOU?

As a young adult, your chances of using alcohol and drugs are very high. For many reasons, teenage drinking has increased rapidly in the past year. It is harder for most of you to decide what you are going to do about drinking because many of your parents drink, and they don't consider alcohol a "drug." And because alcohol is legal, it appears safer to you than other drugs.

Let's go over some of the reasons others might bring up if they talk to you about alcohol and drugs. It is hardly fair to speak only of dependent or ill people using drugs when millions of persons use these same substances without becoming dependent.

One key reason already mentioned for using drugs and alcohol is pleasure. There is no way of denying that certain drugs add to a person's feeling of enjoyment and relaxation. Your personal choice to drink or to take drugs to increase pleasure and enjoyment can be a most important decision. Which drug or alcoholic beverage would you select for this purpose? How much of the drug or alcohol would you take? In what situations or with which people would you do this experimentation? Finally, how much do you know about the short- and long-range effects of this drug on your mind and body?

These questions may seem silly or unimportant to you. After all, you simply want to feel good or relaxed and this shouldn't involve a lot of questions or the reading of books. Taking a drink, popping a pill, or smoking marijuana just isn't that big a deal. Must someone think and analyze everything he or she does just to have a little fun and enjoyment?

No, you don't have to question everything. It is your body, your life, your future, and your happiness. So long as you do not restrict the freedom of others or injure them, you have a tremendous amount of freedom. This is especially true in a drug culture such as ours that offers multiple drug experiences to individuals throughout their lifetime. However, because of this fact you should consider the following questions when you consider using drugs or alcohol for pleasure in social or recreational settings.

QUESTIONS FOR PERSONAL DECISION MAKING

1. What do you know about the particular drug or alcoholic beverage? What category of drugs does it

fall under? How does it affect the brain and the body?

2. How long do the effects of this drug or alcoholic beverage last? What minimal amounts of this drug or alcohol bring about the effect that you wish, and is there a danger in taking more than a specific amount of this drug?

3. What occurs when this drug or alcohol is mixed with another drug or alcoholic beverage? Does it increase the feeling you desired, or does it result in an entirely different feeling and sensation?

4. Are there legal penalties attached to the use of this drug or alcohol? If so, are these penalties enforced? What are your chances of being arrested?

5. Where will you be and who will be present when you take this drug or alcohol? Will these people help or protect you if the need should arise?

6. How much does the drug or alcohol block, distort, alter, or change your perception of reality? Does the drug or alcohol allow you to maintain sufficient contact with reality and not limit your capacity to deal with emergencies?

7. Is your choice of a drug or alcohol a substance that is an addictive chemical? In other words, have you selected a substance that over time could cause your body to require this chemical for daily functioning?

8. Do you have friends who have successfully used this type of drug or alcohol with no ill effects? If so, will they be present when you experiment?

9. What's in it for you? What kind of feelings do you wish to have as a result of taking this drug or alcoholic beverage? Why are these feelings important for you to experience?

USING DRUGS AND ALCOHOL
FOR PROBLEM SOLVING

Although today's use of drugs and alcohol for social and recreational purposes is a new and unsettled issue, the use of these substances for problem solving is quite old. At the turn of the twentieth century the largest number of addicts in this country were women between twenty and forty years of age. This probably began with the wide distribution of patent and drugstore medicines following the Civil War. Women in small towns and farming areas were the victims of peddlers selling "medicines" containing a mixture of opium and alcohol.

The woman who purchased these patent medicines was usually a person desiring some relief from the fatigue of life in nineteenth-century America. These patent medicines offered some help to the tired and exhausted, but the price they paid was an addiction to a powerful narcotic drug. The problem was eventually resolved by the passage of the Pure Food and Drug Act in 1906, which regulated the interstate sale of unsafe and misbranded food and drugs.

Relief from pain, fatigue, and physical discomfort is only one example of the use of drugs and alcohol as a means of solving or aiding personal problems. In fact, the use of drugs to aid in helping a person deal with physical distress is easily understood. What is often difficult to understand is the same use of drugs and alcohol to solve problems arising from emotional and social concerns.

Examples of individuals using drugs and alcohol to solve personal problems unrelated to physical causes are numerous. Think for a moment of the number of friends and acquaintances you know who are somewhat shy, timid, or uncertain of themselves. What would they say at a party if you offered them something to make them more relaxed and at ease with other people? If they said, "Yes," and accepted marijuana or alcohol, it might well relax them and make them more comfortable. The question is, would they then use these chemicals as a way of life whenever they felt uncertain of other people and situations? Would the drug or alcohol in time become a substitute for the "real" person they are or might have been?

Other examples of problem solving through drug and

alcohol use could range from persons using pep pills to cut their appetites so they can lose weight, to unhappy and lonely individuals finding a secret fantasy world through drugs, to persons with economic pressures wishing a temporary escape through alcohol or drugs, to the unemployed seeking relief by any means available. For all these people, and a great many more, drugs and alcohol hold some promise for getting out from under the pressures and tensions of life. They also shut out, for however short a period, the feelings we all have sometimes of helplessness, unhappiness, and inadequacy in certain situations.

The question all of us must face in using drugs and alcohol to solve personal problems is easy to say but difficult to recognize and resolve. The question is, "Do drugs and alcohol really assist us in dealing with personal problems or do they simply help us in temporarily getting around the problem?" If they do not actually aid us in handling personal problems, then an additional question must be answered. "Do drugs, over a long period of time, help in solving problems, or do they create new problems, possibly more serious than the earlier problem they were used to solve?"

CAN DRUGS AND ALCOHOL INCREASE KNOWLEDGE ABOUT ONE'S SELF?

A final use of drugs and alcohol is concerned with how these substances might aid us in better understanding our self. The use of drugs and alcohol for this purpose has been reported by many people actually using many drugs, and is not an easy question to answer. After all, what works for one person may not work for another. It is very hard to dispute or question what someone else has actually experienced under the influence of drugs or alcohol.

In thinking of how drugs and alcohol might create new forms of personal knowledge, it is important to remember one major fact about drugs and alcohol. *Neither drugs nor alcohol create new problems of nervous system activity.* In other words, whatever type of drug or alcohol used, the chemical in and of itself does not create or originate any form of knowledge or information you do not already possess.

What drugs and alcohol do when they appear to offer us new experiences or new pieces of knowledge is to alter or change our usual process of thinking. This change can occur in many ways, but basically drugs and alcohol act on how we perceive the environment around us. If a drug intensifies or heightens our visual or auditory senses, then we do indeed see and hear things differently. If, on the other hand, the drug mutes or dulls our visual or auditory powers, then this too affects what we normally see or hear.

Drugs and alcohol also affect our memories. Under the influence of these substances we may remember things we had long forgotten or our memories may seem to change. If on the one hand we therefore find our memories different through drugs or alcohol—and we add to this a new way of experiencing the environment—then certainly it appears that new information and knowledge can be gained from drugs and alcohol.

A question at this point often raised by persons against the use of drugs and alcohol goes something like this: "Aren't there other experiences far safer and more powerful than drugs and alcohol for gaining new forms of knowledge? What of Yoga, hypnosis, religion, psychotherapy, meditation, and other means of arriving at new personal information? Aren't these equally of use to you and less dangerous and harmful?"

This question must be considered by anyone seriously using drugs and alcohol as a major means of increasing his or her knowledge about him- or herself. A final question for anyone using drugs and alcohol for any reason is related to his or her own survival as a member of society. This question is simply, *"How does the drug or alcohol you use—especially if you use it*

*over an extended period of time—affect your relation-
ships with your friends, family, and society?"*

The answer to this question must be yours. No one
else can answer it for you. It is an honest and serious
question, and you might need additional help before
you actually feel confident in your answer. The references and books that follow might be of help in deciding this question.

FURTHER READINGS

Alberle, D. F. *The Peyote Religion Among the Navajo.*
Chicago: Aldine Publisher, 1966. An anthropologist
studies the use of peyote among the Navajo and how
this drug is used in religious ritual.

Burroughs, W. *Speed.* New York: Olympia Press,
1970. The world of the speed freak as seen in a
humorous portrayal of one young person on the
move.

Childress, A. *A Hero Ain't Nothing but a Sandwich.*
New York: Coward-McCann, 1973. The story of a
thirteen-year-old heroin addict told from his point of
view and those who knew him best.

Cole, R. *The Grass Pipe.* Boston: Little, Brown and
Company, 1969. A novel by an outstanding psychiatrist about young teens and their early experiences
in using marijuana.

Craddock, W. J. *Be Not Content.* New York: Double-
day, 1970. A novel depicting the extensive drug culture in California at the height of the psychedelic
revolution.

Fleming, A. *Alcohol: The Delightful Poison.* New
York: Delacorte Press, 1975. A historical overview
of alcohol from the earliest times to the present.

Goldstein, R. *The Poetry of Rock.* New York: Bantam
Books, 1969. The effect of drugs through reprint of
seventy folk and rock songs and a discussion on their
impact on American society.

Gustaitis, R. *Turning On.* New York: Macmillan,

1969. A writer who traveled across the country to discover alternative ways for young people to "turn on" without drugs discusses his findings.

Harris, J. *Junkie Priest*. New York: Pocket Books, 1970. A priest among the world of addicts and drug abusers.

Huxley, A. *The Doors of Perception* and *Heaven and Hell*. New York: Harper and Row, 1956. A noted author and scientist writes of his own experiences in taking the drug mescaline.

Schulman, L. M., ed. *The Loners: Short Stories About the Young and Alienated*. New York: Macmillan, 1970. A collection of well-known short stories centered around the theme of alienation.

SPIRITUAL CHOICES

Discovering Your Spirituality

BY JOYCE SLAYTON MITCHELL

Spirituality is sweeping the country. Church attendance may be down in the 1970s but the meditation groups, Eastern religious groups, traveling gurus, and psychic consciousness groups are booming. From TM (Transcendental Meditation grounded by guru Maharishi Mahesh Yogi) that claims six hundred thousand U.S. meditators who meditate forty minutes a day in order to feel better to a totally religious community such as Hare Krishna and back again to feeling better with bioenergetics is a great range of groups which taken altogether form an unsurpassed spiritual movement.

Who needs them? Why now? What are they like? How do they differ? These are the questions of religious leaders, observers of behavior and culture, and the psychologists and psychiatrists who also try to make people feel better.

Some observers of the spiritual movement have felt that people need someone to tell them how to set things right—tell them what to do. It doesn't matter to them what they do as long as they find peace of mind, or less strife and stress, and less negative energy in their daily lives. Religious leaders have said that people are reacting to the human feeling of alienation from the world. They are seeking a spiritual answer—a longing for at-oneness with something greater than humankind—something beyond the secular, a union with their source.

Even though there may be a basic human need for spirituality, different human needs are met by different groups. While some promote the glorification of the seeker (est) others give up self for the glorification of God (Hare Krishna). Some are religious and come directly from Hinduism (Meher Baba, the Divine Light, and Hare Krishna) or Islam (Sufi), or Buddhism (the gurus). Some are religious with their own prophet (Baha'i faith). Others make a point of saying they are *not* religious: TM (although it borrows words and symbols from Hinduism), est, Arica, the psychic consciousness, and bioenergetic groups.

The spirituality movement may have been caused by an alienating and lonely world; it may have come because of the lack of spirituality in our secular churches and synagogues. Whatever the reason for its thriving popularity right now, for most people, joining a spiritual or meditation group is a search for some form of spirituality in their lives. That is, *a longing for communion with the source* (God, Spiritual Force, Energy, Life-Force, Truth) *and mystery of life.* Religion has always been the traditional answer for integrating spirituality with a person's intellectual, sexual, emotional, and social development in order to realize his or her wholeness. But when institutional religion fails, as it has in the lives of many, a person often seeks this communion with the source and mystery of life through other sources such as meditation, chanting, singing, and dancing as found in Eastern religions and meditation groups.

A yearning for the mystical and religious experience can be fulfilled by the Yoga Hindu gurus through exercises and meditation. Through the many Buddhist meditation groups of Zen and Tibetan who teach great discipline for the final union with ultimate reality. The Arica group unifies the body, mind, and emotions with meditation and exercise while searching for the "Essential Self." The Sufi, an Islam group, meditates and dances simple folk dances, while the Hare Krishna sings, dances, and chants to bring out the dormant love of

God by serving and glorifying him from a Hindu perspective. Another Hindu group is Meher Baba, that has meditation and love study groups. Still another is the Divine Light which differs from many others because it meets emergency needs of people, such as their need for food, clothing, and shelter in addition to Hindu meditation. The Jesus movement comes from the spiritual movement. Many traditional Christian churches have been influenced by the Eastern religious and meditation groups.

In opposition to the religions that ask one to do for others, or to give up self, is the est group that tells people what to do in obscene language in two weekends but ends up telling them to be totally responsible for self and not to waste energy worrying about others (the poor, oppressed, and the sick). With this release of guilt for the violence in the world and energy used for caring for others, the person will have new energy to do anything he or she wills for himself or herself. Others who work in creating new energy are the alpha-wave training and hypnosis groups, as well as bioenergetics that eliminate nervous tension. They free people from disease and illness by training their brain to control their body. *Psychic consciousness* uses trance to reach present and past lives for healing and curing purposes.

Why are all of those adults just learning that growing up into full personhood includes spiritual growth? You may wonder what it is that keeps so many people from seeking and accepting their spirituality sooner.

Becoming a person isn't easy. Becoming altogether is often a struggle against someone putting us in a clear-cut category, in a box. With that box goes a label, and with the label go all the particular personality traits that fit the name on the label. People are grouped into male or female, black or white, young or old, rich or poor, and worldly or spiritual. Once we are in one category we are treated as if we were all alike . . . regardless of the "me." When we get into one of these boxes or categories, like others, we start becoming "against" the other end of the scale. As a result male against female becomes sexism, white against black becomes racism, young against old become agism, and worldly against spiritual becomes secularism.

Being secular in our behavior means that we believe that if we can improve our human condition enough we will have a better world. It leaves out the spiritual needs of a person. Secularism in our religious institutions is illustrated by their preoccupation with social action programs for racial justice and economic equality *in place of* communion with the source of life. Many of our religious institutions keep God in their buildings and within the power of the white male clergy. In this secular way our spiritual life remains outside of us rather than a living or working part of our very being.

Secularism leads to separating the physical and spiritual within us. Separation, polarization, and alienation are all terms used to describe opposites going further apart. The behavior of opposites and polarized people is exploitation as one group tries to get the better of the other, and the consequence is hate or apathy.

In order to become a person, to be altogether, we must accept the spirituality within us (not necessarily the Sunday school version of spirituality out there or up above us) and say that we are indeed spiritual beings, just as we are sexual beings, intellectual beings, aging beings, and emotional beings.

To be whole means to include everything you experience about yourselves—not always the obvious or what you talk about, or what society says males are. When society insists that males always be in control, independent, and cool, and a young man is in the process of seeking security, being dependent, and expressing his feelings, he often goes through stages of thinking that there is something wrong with him. He thinks that what he sees in himself cannot be true and that other people in his group aren't like he is—he doesn't fit the label on the box, the sex-role stereotype. He isn't what "boys" are like. And if he has learned from our society that a real man doesn't need religion, then he will never know how spirituality is a part of his nature.

Recognizing and accepting your spirituality isn't only for you who go to traditional churches. It is also for you who have learned your religion through the teachings of Hinduism, Buddhism, or Islam, and for you who have been turned off from your childhood religion or have been brought up without religion and have never noticed that you are a spiritual being.

As you begin to learn about yourself, or who you are and what you can do, then you can be free enough to notice where our secular world is leading you. When you start to see what is in store for you: cars, radios, stereos, most popular dates, summer trips, clothes, allowances, top man on the team, you may begin to whisper to yourself, Is this all there is? Is this what making it is all about?

When the secular stereotype becomes a reality, then you look at what you are like and ask, What else is there? What are the possibilities in me? What can I be? Who is the man I can become? What is my nature? It is now that you may turn toward your spiritual possibilities. The last thing. After you have tried becoming a person only on society's idea of what is masculine, and on society's secular terms, and seen it and found it and bought it and said . . . this *is* all there is! You finally learn that you can *not* live an abundant life with others: one with love and joy and strength, and gentleness and assertiveness, with justice and mercy within grace . . . by bread alone!

A Religious Choice

Religion is a lot like men's liberation. Many men wonder why anyone would want it. It's understandable why some people flocked to religion—slaves, peasants, women, children, the poor and the handicapped—they hoped to transcend their difficult world to get to another. And it's easy to understand why women want liberation—to get out from under their unequal and unfair treatment in a male dominated society.

But why would men want to be free from a power position? Why would men who dominate women want men's liberation? And why would a man who has control of his place in this world turn to religion? Most don't. But some do. Some male liberationists have learned that the power they feel isn't as free as it appears to be. It has limits. The dominance and control you have over females is yours because you accept a controlling system. Yet as soon as you accept your control over others, you in turn can be controlled *by* others. The price of controlling other people, rather than an equal partnership with others, is that your classmates, your brothers, and later the men you work with will always be in fierce competition with you to be on top, to be making it, to have just a little bit more power than you have. The very power system that says you must be the boss in your relationships with young women is the same system that pits your brothers against you.

Constant competition is devastating. It prevents you from realizing close friendships, from honestly expressing your feelings, your needs, your frights, your joys. It prevents you from accepting your natural dependencies on others. In other words, the male sex role which appears to be so important to you is the very thing that controls you— you are manipulated by the male stereotype. Your competitiveness and need to come off as if you were in total control over others are well understood by business and corporations as they later bribe you with promotions, prestige, money, and a chance to be boss. Warren Farrell points out in *The Liberated Man* that you may not know how you are manipulated but advertising knows how and its profits are based on it.

Like male liberation, religion can show you some of the myths of materialistic power and the high cost of controlling other people.

To understand your full human potential, you must broaden your concept of a male person so that your wholeness includes being dependent, expressing your feelings, and sharing in relationships as well as recognizing male stereotypes of control, of independence, and of coolness. In his chapter, "Jesus the Liberator," Professor Leonard Swidler writes that Jesus rejected the false division of traits by sex in order to demonstrate his fully human personality. Swidler illustrates with Scripture how Jesus combined the so-called male characteristic of reason with feelings, of firmness with gentleness, of justice with mercy, of pride with humility, and of provider with need for security. Developing a complete range of human characteristics rather than a narrow definition of masculinity is liberation. Marnin Kligfeld, in his chapter, "The Jewish Choice," invites you to reject the definition of yourself as only a materialistic person and to demand to be a fully human being, integrating your spirituality with your reasoning, your feelings, and your secular world.

Jesus the Liberator

BY LEONARD SWIDLER

I was struck when reading a description of a liberated man by how much it sounded like a description of Jesus. I doubt there are many men in the history of the world who could be called examples of "liberated men." So it would be worth the effort to see what the life of Jesus could teach us about being liberated men.

It doesn't matter if we are believing Christians or not. What I am talking about is the historical Jesus, the man who lived and died on that small patch of land today called Palestine by some and Israel by others. Some of the greatest and most world-changing wisdom has come out of that land in the past, and much more is waiting for us there today and in the future if we will only look. In this case the place to look is the life of the Jew, Jesus.

The only reliable documents we have that tell us something about the life of Jesus are the four Gospels. These Gospels, however, are not the straight factual reports of eyewitnesses of the events in the life of Jesus of Nazareth as one might find in the columns of *The New York Times*. Rather they are four different faith statements reflecting at least four primitive Christian communities that believed that Jesus was the Messiah, the Lord, the Savior of the world. They were composed from a variety of sources, written and oral, over a

period of time and in response to certain needs felt in
the communities and individuals at the time; consequently, even though the Gospels are in general har-
mony, they are many layered. Nevertheless, with careful
scholarship we can get a pretty good picture of what
Jesus did and said in those situations which have been
recorded. But there are many things about Jesus that
the Gospel writers did not think important enough to
report on. So we will have to be content with some
gaps in our picture.

Secondly, Christians take Jesus to be a model of how
to live a fully *human* life, not just a male life. Ancient
Christians made the point clear in the Nicene Creed
(A.D. 325) when they said of Jesus, "et *homo* factus
est," " and he became *human*." They did *not* say, "et
vir factus est," "and he became *male*." Hence for
Christians the heart of Jesus' "Gospel," his "Good
News," is for everyone, women, men and children alike.
Nevertheless, because, what ever else he was, Jesus was
a male human being, his life will also have a particular
kind of message for other male humans. Put briefly, if
Jesus was a real man, his way of acting or speaking
cannot be called unmanly.

In our society, and in most others as well, we have
for thousands of years been saying that certain ways
of acting, thinking, and speaking are specifically manly
and their opposites are womanly. (1) Men are supposed to be reasonable and cool; women are supposed
to be persons of feeling and emotion; (2) men are to be
firm and aggressive; women, gentle and peaceful; (3)
men should be advocates of justice; women, mercy;
(4) men should have pride and self-confidence; women
should have humility and reserve; (5) men are said to
be the providers of security (food, clothing, shelter);
women, the ones who need security; (6) men are supposed to be concerned with organization and structure;
women, with persons, especially children.

From what we know of Jesus, in which of these
divisions did he fit?

I. REASONABLE AND COOL: FEELING AND EMOTION

Jesus had a large number of vigorous, at times even extremely vicious enemies, both in debate and in life and death situations. In debate: After Jesus criticized the chief priests and scribes, ". . . they watched him, and sent spies, who pretended to be sincere, that they might take hold of what he said, so as to deliver him up to the authority and jurisdiction of the governor. They asked him, 'Teacher, we know that you speak and teach rightly, and show no partiality, but truly teach the way of God. Is it lawful for us to give tribute to Caesar, or not?' " They were a clever lot, for Israel was occupied by Roman troops and the Jews in general consequently hated everything Roman with a passion, and especially the publicans (native tax collectors for Rome). If Jesus said straight out to pay Roman taxes, he would have immediately lost his influence with people, which would have suited his enemies. But if he said do not pay taxes, he would have immediately ended up in a Roman jail, or perhaps worse, which also would have suited his enemies.

"But he perceived their craftiness, and said to them, 'Show me a coin. Whose likeness and inscription has it?' They said, 'Caesar's.' He said to them, 'Then render to Caesar the things that are Caesar's, and to God the things that are God's.' " A most *reasonable* response. "And they were not able in the presence of the people to catch him by what he said; but marveling at his answer they were silent" (Luke 20:20–26).*

In life and death situations: "When they heard this, all in the synagogue were filled with wrath. And they rose and put him out of the city, and led him to the brow of the hill on which their city was built, that they might throw him down headlong." Jesus' reaction?

---

* Scripture quotations are from the Revised Standard Version.

"But passing through the midst of them he went away" (Luke 4:28–30). Real *cool.*

More examples could be given, but these place Jesus in the "masculine" camp for category I.

On the other hand, when Jesus visited his friends Martha and Mary, two sisters, he learned that their brother Lazarus had died. Mary came to Jesus and "when Jesus saw her weeping, and the Jews who came with her also weeping, he was deeply moved in spirit and troubled; and he said, 'Where have you laid him?' They said to him, 'Lord, come and see.' Jesus wept. So the jews said, 'See how he loved him!' " (John 11:33–36). Jesus was clearly a person with deep emotions, and showed them publicly.

Hence, it would seem that in category I, Jesus had not only the so-called "masculine" characteristics but also "feminine" ones.

II. FIRM AND AGGRESSIVE: GENTLE AND PEACEFUL

There is no question but that Jesus was *firm.* He certainly was firm when he said to his chief follower, Peter, in front of the rest of his followers: "Get behind me, Satan!" (Mark 8:33). Jesus was most *aggressive* in his verbal attack on his enemies among the scribes and Pharisees. *Six* times in a row he denounced them to their faces as frauds: "But woe to you, scribes and Pharisees, hypocrites!" And he went on: "Woe to you, blind guides! . . . You blind guides, straining out a gnat and swallowing a camel! . . . You serpents, you brood of vipers . . ." (Matt. 23:13–33).

On the other hand Jesus spoke of *gentleness.* With extraordinary gentleness Jesus spoke to the weary and weighted: "Come to me, all who labor and are heavy laden, and I will give you rest. Take my yoke upon you and learn from me; for I am gentle and lowly in heart, and you will find rest for your souls. For my yoke is easy, and my burden is light" (Matt. 11:28–30).

If one word could sum up the life and message of Jesus, that word might be peace, *shalom*. Time and again when Jesus healed someone he said, "Your faith has saved you; go in peace" (Luke 7:50; see also 8:48; Mark 5:34). He promised much to the peace-makers: "Blessed are the peacemakers, for they shall be called sons of God" (Matt. 5:9). To his followers he gives more: "I have said this to you, that in me you may have peace . . . Peace I leave with you, my peace I give to you; not as the world gives do I give you" (John 16:33; 14:27).

Obviously Jesus was firm, aggressive, *and* gentle, peace-loving; in category II he was both "masculine" and "feminine."

III. JUSTICE AND MERCY

Jesus was a strong advocate of justice. To be just is to do what is right, and in a society it is to follow the law. Jesus insisted on scrupulously following the law. "Think not that I have come to abolish the law and the prophets; I have come not to abolish them but to fulfill them. For truly, I say to you, till heaven and earth pass away, not an iota, not a dot will pass from the law until all is accomplished" (Matt. 5:17–18).

Several times Jesus spoke of the last judgment—where final justice would be meted out. "So it will be at the close of the age. The angels will come out and separate the evil from the righteous, and throw them into the furnace of fire, [where there will be weeping and gnashing of teeth]" (Matt. 13:49–50).

But in the matter of mercy and forgiveness Jesus went beyond all his predecessors—and successors. He preached the unheard-of doctrine of loving one's enemies. "You have heard that it was said, 'You shall love your neighbor and hate your enemy.' But I say to you, Love your enemies and pray for those who persecute you" (Matt. 5:43–44). Fantastic words! And Jesus *did* just that at the most critical moment of his life—his death. "And when they came to the place called The Skull, there they crucified him, and the criminals, one on the right and one on the left. And Jesus said, 'Father, forgive them; for they know not what they do'" (Luke 23:33–34). To the bitter end, Jesus was a man of mercy.

As in the first two categories, so also in this, Jesus strongly exemplified both the "masculine" and "feminine" traits. Jesus was a person of both justice and mercy, and forgiveness.

IV. PRIDE AND SELF-CONFIDENCE: HUMILITY AND RESERVE

There is a proper kind of pride which, like its opposite, humility, is simply truthfulness, affirming the good you see in yourself. A striking example of this pride occurred when Jesus made his triumphant entry into Jerusalem.

The self-assurance and self-confidence Jesus exhibited when dragged before the chief council of Israel was extraordinary. Only in someone who had a very deep grasp on himself could it be found; despite the violence and threats involved, Jesus was clearly in control, in a way that usually happens only in spy thrillers: Jesus stood before Pilate, the notoriously cruel and bloodthirsty Roman governor of the area. The man had the power of release and a vicious death, and yet Jesus had a steel control over himself—and his judge: Pilate said to Jesus, " 'Are you the King of the Jews?' Jesus answered, 'Do you say this of your own accord, or did others say it to you about me?' Pilate answered, 'Am I a Jew? Your own nation and the chief priests have handed you over to me; what have you done?' Jesus answered, 'My kingship is not of this world; if my kingship were of this world, my servants would fight that I might not be handed over to the Jews; but my kingship is not from the world.' Pilate said to him, 'So you are a king?' Jesus answered, 'You say that I am a king. For this I was born, and for this I have come into the world, to bear witness to the truth. Everyone who is of the truth hears my voice.' '. . . Do you not know that I have power to release you, and power to crucify you?' Jesus answered, 'You would have no power over me unless it had been given you from above' " (John 18:33–37; 19:10).

And yet, Jesus is, rightly, known for teaching humility.

Jesus spoke of a Pharisee in the Temple who bragged to God about all his virtues, and of a hated tax collector who beat his breast and said, "God, be merciful to me a sinner!" Warning the first man he would not be right with God, Jesus said, "For every one who exalts himself will be humbled, but he who humbles himself will be exalted" (Luke 18:9–14).

Jesus paradoxically also often taught his followers *reserve*. For example, he said, "Beware of practicing your piety before [people] in order to be seen by them . . ." (Matt. 6:1). From this evidence, and still more in the Gospels, we would have to conclude that Jesus combined the so-called "masculine" traits of pride and self-confidence with the supposedly "feminine" characteristics of humility and reserve.

V. PROVIDER OF SECURITY: NEED FOR SECURITY

It was to Jesus that his many followers flocked to find the *security* of the meaning of human life, of whom Peter said, "Lord, to whom shall we go? You have the words of eternal life" (John 6:68); who said of himself, "I am the bread of life; he who comes to me shall not hunger" (John 6:35). Yet it was also the same Jesus who sent his disciples out with "no purse, no bag, no sandals" (Luke 10:4); who said to them, "Therefore I tell you, do not be anxious about your life, what you

shall eat, nor about your body, what you shall put on"
(Luke 12:22); who said of himself, "Foxes have holes,
and birds of the air have nests, but the Son of Man has
nowhere to lay his head" (Luke 9:58), and who in
the end felt a crushing need for security in his God:
"My God, my God, why hast thou forsaken me?"
(Mark 15:34). Jesus both provided, and needed, security.

VI. ORGANIZATION: PEOPLE

In the final category, note Jesus' concern with *organization and structure* by recalling how carefully he
chose his followers, his apostles—twelve to match
symbolically the twelve tribes of Israel ("You will sit
on thrones judging the twelve tribes of Israel" [Luke
22:30]), the painful and painstaking instruction of his
followers, his sending out of the seventy disciples like
lead men in a campaign today "to all the towns and
places where he himself was about to come" (Luke
10:1). But there is also Jesus' intense concern with
individual persons, his healing of numerous miserable
people, lepers, blind, lame, and paralytics, even the
dead (!), his affection for despised individuals, like the
tax collector Zacchaeus (Luke 19:1 ff.), the "adulter-
ous woman" (John 8:1 ff.)—note Jesus' reaching out
particularly to women, a class especially looked down
on in his society. There is also Jesus' special concern
for *children*—in fact, the holding of them up as a
model: "Truly, I say to you, whoever does not receive
the [reign] of God like a child shall not enter it." "And
he took them in his arms and blessed them, laying his
hands upon them" (Mark 10:15–16).

CONCLUSION

There is no question. The evidence shows over-
whelmingly that Jesus had the full range of "feminine"

and "masculine" characteristics in all the categories. What conclusion does that suggest? For one, it suggests that the division of characteristics by sex is quite artificial. Jesus would have been less than a full human being if he had only the so-called masculine set. In fact this sex role distortion has too often happened to the *image* of Jesus in Christianity, past and present. At different times and places Jesus has been seen solely as the great ruler of the world and stern, just judge whose favor must be curried through his more sympathetic Mother. At other times and places Jesus has been projected as all-feeling, "loving," or, according to the Jesus freaks, a person who saves, without any just judgment involved. But Jesus in fact was not just masculine or just feminine, but he was a full human being.

What has often happened to the *image* of Jesus in our society also tends to happen to most of us to a greater or lesser degree. We men are made to think we must cultivate only our "manly" traits, and avoid our "womanly" ones. But the message, the God-spel, of Jesus is that to be a "real man," a "real human"—to be really liberated—we must reject the false division of traits by sex and become full human persons. Jesus said, "I am . . . the truth . . ." (John 14:6), and "the truth will make you free" (John 8:32).

The Jewish Choice

BY MARNIN KLIGFELD

There are hundreds, if not thousands, of ways to be Jewish. In fact there are probably as many ways to be Jewish as there are Jews. There are Jews who are secular, religious, leftist, rightist, Zionist, Yiddishist, agnostic, gastronomic, and of course, Orthodox, Conservative, and Reform. This is a strength in Judaism; each and every one of these Jews is as much a Jew as the other. We all choose to express our Jewishness differently. Our concern here is the spiritual Jewish choice or the religious choice, a choice which is particularly difficult in our age.

In writing about the spiritual Jewish choice, I do not pretend to be an authority; I do not have the answers. In fact, I don't believe that anyone has the answers for anyone else. We all make spiritual choices for ourselves, and I would be wary of anyone who pretends to have the final word. My own spirituality as a Jew is a real problem for me. The most I can do is to share my struggle, share what I have found meaningful for me, and invite you to struggle and work at living a religious existence in a secular world.

I learned much of what I am writing here from a classroom of twenty-one high-school students very much like yourselves. When I first walked into their classroom, I thought that I had a lot to teach and that I had exciting ideas to share. But something was wrong; I could not get their attention. They all looked bored, as if they were challenging me to entertain them. What I didn't realize was that in many ways the twenty-one students in the room knew much more than I, although they couldn't verbalize what they knew. Until then I thought that teaching had to do with me as a teacher teaching and they as students learning. What I did not realize, and what I later learned, was that the group of us did not exist in a vacuum. We existed within a building, within an institution, within a community, within a country, within a culture, all of which had a profound influence on what was to take place in that classroom. They were all in the classroom with us though I didn't see them at first. I hated teaching that year since I got nowhere in the traditional sense of covering material. Yet, it turned out that I learned more there than in many years as a student.

This particular classroom was in an upper-middle-class suburban synagogue. The synagogue building itself was extremely lavish and was constructed by a famous architect. When I saw the building and the classroom for the first time, I saw a beautiful setting in which to teach. When the students saw the building and the classroom, they saw a synagogue that stood as a symbol for a great many things beyond a beautiful building. They saw a beautiful but empty facade that stood for values of acquisition and materialism. This was a living lesson to them that the organized Jewish community had chosen to accept a particular part of American culture: to build big, to build lavish, to build the best. They chose to expend tremendous energy into building and maintaining a facade, but they were too tired to breathe life into it. My students knew this problem from their own homes, where to a greater or lesser degree, their parents had worked hard all their lives to provide their children with what they never had. Unfortunately, many were too tired when they got home at night to offer what was really needed—themselves. Knowing this, and seeing the huge synagogue as more of the same, they hated that facade, that lie, because they knew its emptiness.

The synagogue was once a small covenant among a

group of people and their God, which offered warmth and a circle of affection through which people could find direction and meaning in their lives. It was once a source of the highest human values. I believe that the synagogue today can still stand as a reminder that we are all individuals within a community. It should be there to remind us of the values that transcend the mercantilism of today. It can be a source of energy, aimed at uplifting humankind in a world that crushes people all too easily. Within the synagogue, the religious school is the mechanism for passing on the essence of Jewish life.

My students saw school (including religious school) as a place to be indoctrinated into the values of our culture. They heard me talking about the importance of human beings and human values, but they saw me standing in a building that cost far too much money, that exhibited far too much lavish decor, and through whose halls walked too many people clad in clothing that was far too expensive. They watched what we did, not what we said. They learned well the lesson that things are more important than people. Whatever I could say would not lessen their horror at learning this particular lesson from people they loved. I came believing that school was to be a place where we shared thoughts, where we learned to think, and learned to be close to one another. The students were coming from a high-school experience in which they learned not to be imaginative, not to be creative, but to disregard their heritage and their dreams, and to disregard their own uniqueness as special individuals. They saw school as a place to learn how to become strangers to themselves, to be stripped of anything that was uniquely their own, and to learn to fit themselves into one of the few molds our society offers. School was a place to limit choices rather than to multiply them. They saw religious school as the same process taking place in the synagogue.

But the synagogue was to be a place of inner values where people could stand in relation to their God. What happened? What killed the spirit of the synagogue? The answer to these questions came slowly since they are broader and more far-reaching than I expected. I realized that the synagogue along with the rest of our society is based upon control by the rational intellect. We learn to dominate experience rather than to involve ourselves in experience. In a totally rationalistic framework, all openness to new things, to wonder, to mystery, to excitement, to love, to immersing ourselves in experience is lost. Without these, religion dies and becomes a narrow, cold, rationalistic explanation of historical events. This robs religion of its breath, of its very soul. In this model, Judaism cannot be a wellspring of life and values.

A Hasidic Tale, as told by Elie Wiesel

When the great Rabbi Israel Baal Shem Tov saw misfortune threatening the Jews, it was his custom to go to a certain part of the forest to meditate. There he would light a fire and say a special prayer. The miracle would be accomplished and the misfortune averted. Later when his disciple, the celebrated Magid of Mezritch had occasion, for the same reason, to intercede with Heaven, he would go to the same place in the forest and say, "Master of the Universe, listen. I do not know how to light the fire but I am still able to say the prayer." Again, the miracle was accomplished. Still later Rabbi Moshe Leib of Sasov, in order to save his people, once more would go into the forest and say, "I do not know how to light the fire, I do not know the prayer, but I know the place and this must be sufficient." It was sufficient and the miracle was accomplished. Then it fell to Rabbi Israel of Rizhyn to overcome misfortune. Sitting in his armchair, his head in his hands, he spoke to God. "I am unable to light the fire and I do not know the prayer. I cannot even find the place in the forest. All I can do is to tell the story and this must be sufficient." And it was sufficient.*

*From Elie Wiesel, *Gates of the Forest* (New York: Avon, 1966).

I strongly disagree with this tale. Merely to tell the story is not enough. If it were, I would not be writing, for the spiritual choice would be open to all. Instead, the life of the spirit is a well-guarded secret. Our mission is to learn how to light the fire of our spirits and to kindle our prayers. Prayer without the fire is empty. Fire without the prayer is lost.

I came to see that the mink coats in the synagogue pews were there for a good reason. I saw people separate their lives in the sanctuary from their lives outside. Inside they would dress themselves in beautiful clothing with beautiful jewelry and come and mouth the words of the prayers, but outside they lived as though they had never said those words. It struck me that I had read of this conflict before. I searched until I found the same idea written a long time ago, about a different synagogue, about a different place of worship.

Your sacred festivals, I hate them, scorn them. Your sacrifices, I will not smell their smoke. You offer me your gifts, I will not take them. You offer fatted cattle, I will not look at them. No more of your hymns for me, I will not listen to your lutes. No, let justice well up like fresh water, let honesty roll in full tide. Was it sacrifice and offering you brought me, all the forty years within the desert? Seek to be honest, not evil, so live that the eternal may be with you, as you think He is. I hate evil and love honesty. Set justice up again. It may be that the Eternal, the God of Hosts, may pity those left in the house of Joseph.

Amos 5:21

I believe that by going along with the dominant values in our culture, the religious establishments, and in this context the synagogue, have done an unamendable wrong. The synagogue is the place that must offer a relighting of the timeless values that transcend the emptiness we see all around us. Not only is the synagogue no fountain of values, but it even refuses to cry

out at the abominations of our day. Even mass destruc-
tion through war passes unchallenged, because none of
us has any subjective standard of reality with which to
oppose the lies we are told. We have no grounding,
no inner ear, we are cut off from our own hearts.

My aim here is not to blame, because there is no one
to blame. There is a subtle interplay among us all,
among the people, the synagogue, and the rabbis, that
has contributed to our deaths as spiritual beings. We
are all involved so we are all responsible. Somehow
we have been persuaded that the joy in life is found
only in power, in status, in popularity, in achievements,
and in the rational mind. By accepting that point of
view, we've lost the awe, the mystery, the wonder, the
helplessness, the dread and the magic the world has to
offer. Given this fact, our society has become alienated
and impoverished, cut off from its life source. The
synagogue has failed in that it has accepted these values
and not stood up for the true life of the spirit. My
anger with the synagogue and with our society is based
on their construction of narrow molds of acceptable
life-styles. They have chosen to barrage all of us and
convince us of who we are. They have tried to set out
roads and patterns and ways of living that are acceptable, and to funnel us through those particular
ways. Somehow there is no voice in our society calling
for values aside from personal gain. We allow ourselves
to be convinced that becoming rich is what life is
about, and then we give ourselves over to that goal. I
believe that the role of religion and the role of the
synagogue is to help us all to get in touch with who
we really are, to experience ourselves and the world
and to stand in relation to God.

During services, I sat with a class of students and
we saw the emptiness written on the faces of the con-
gregants, their parents. They know these "successful"
people. They lived through marriages breaking up that
had been built on mutual need and not love. They knew
the cynicism and the despair in some of the richest
homes in America, and they knew the emptiness of a

life with no grounding, with no centeredness, with no sense of self. They know that a society that grinds the poor and is run for the benefit of the rich is lacking in any freedom or democracy that it might mouth. They know the wars we fight and they know why we fight them.

We do have a source of values above those of our society. We do have a well at which to drink, and that well is the relationship each of us has with God. When I speak of relationship with God, I talk about that knowledge which one knows at some deep level. I talk about the spirituality that hundreds of people feel crying to them within themselves, for which they can find no expression in their homes or hometown or synagogue. Some people refuse to turn themselves off, refuse to bind themselves into the secular modes of today. They are then caught between their own inner reality and their surroundings. At these times, some pack their bags and go to India or some other Mecca. There they seek for someone to confirm their spiritual needs. The fact that they have to leave their homes and synagogues to travel thousands of miles in order to find some kind of balm for their spirits is a tremendously painful one and virulent indictment of the emptiness of normative religious life in America. But these people are the exception. Most of us go on struggling at home.

When I speak of knowing God, I use knowing in the Biblical sense. The Hebrew word is *ladaat, yada.* The word is used to mean reception into the soul, it means standing in relation to, it means "union with." This union points to the unity of all things. We suffer from the mind-body split that our society has chosen. Somehow we are going to have to realize that the two are one. What is needed is an inner identification with God, rather than dedication to ceremonies.

For I desire steadfast love and not sacrifice.
Daat of God, rather than burnt offerings.
                                        Josea 6:6

Daat of God has intellectual as well as emotional meaning. Daat Elohim is awareness of God, not knowledge
about God. In fact, emotional identification with God
is the central religious postulate, and in the religious
framework, it is the lack of knowledge of God, this
Daat Elohim, that is our downfall. It is this identification with God which the Prophets speak of as the
source of values, as the source of existence and of
spiritual nourishment. We are very far from being personally open to the presence and emotion of God, from
that feeling which is the opposite of emotional solitude.
It is this that we have lost in our rationalistic society.

I find it very difficult to write about the religious experience since it is such a personal phenomenon. Even
more importantly, I cannot write as a Zen master who
"knows." I have had only glimpses or fleeting feelings
of God close to me. Sometimes I have that feeling
around the Sabbath table singing with friends. Sometimes when I am dancing I seem to step beyond the
frenzy of the dance, into relation with something more.
I'm not sure, for it is very hazy. But it is powerful and
compelling. Those few tastes were enough to keep me
searching for another time or place where I felt God's
presence.

The strongest connection for me happened one summer. I was standing in a field on a bright summer
morning, praying and soaking in the day, surrounded by
tall pine trees. My mind was blank, open, receptive, and
I experienced what I can only call a religious experience. I'm not sure though; it is cloudy in my mind. The
daily prayers that I said that morning were different
than any others I had said. Somehow I felt and knew
that I was praying in relation to the Other, not just
standing and saying words. Although it was just a
touch, it was enough to convince me. I suddenly understood the prayers that had been just talk, but that was
years ago and I sometimes wonder if it really happened.

It seems strange that I am trying to invite all of you
to try to explore your own spirituality and relationship
to God. It is so hazy, so ephemeral, but somehow I

know that the connection can be made stronger, that the cloud can be made to leave. Given religious experience as a basis, all the forms take on meaning. Suddenly we know more than just the story, we know how to light the fire.

I want to call you to the viable Jewish model that I know. The model I know is a relational model, a model in which people are partners with God in creating and sustaining the world. It is a model in which people stand over and against God, convenanted to God, very much the way men and women are covenanted in a marriage relationship. Moses stood in relation to God; Abraham argued with God. Rabbi Levi Yitzhak of Berdichev compelled God to stop the persecution of the Jews of his age. The figure of a lonely Jew arguing with the creator of the universe is well known in Jewish literature. This is the life I long for and this is the choice I offer—the struggle to love God with all your heart, with all your soul, and with all your might.

This love relationship with God can imbue ritual with new meaning. The Sabbath, holidays, and every day spent living our Jewishness, whether it be baking challah, lighting candles, drinking wine, or praying, are the expressions of our spirituality as Jews. We live in a secular society, in a society that does not know God, in a society that tries to strip away the spirituality of all of its members. I hope that we do not lose our spirits, that we do not allow ourselves to be channeled or let our choices be cut off. I hope that we demand to be full human beings, emotional, intellectual, and spiritual. But I know the crushing weight of our society, of all the myths, the goals, the values upon which our society is built, and I hope that we will be strong enough to stand up and not to be drawn into the mainstream. I do not mean to say that religion is by definition good and that secular life is by definition bad. What I am trying to say is that the religious establishment of our age, including the Jewish religious establishment, has fallen in among the garbage of our era, and has not stood as a pillar of fire. No one calls us to remain true to ourselves, to remain whole human beings, to keep our spiritual choices open. Therefore it falls on our shoulders, each of us, to guard against the murder of our spirits. Our burden is to reinvigorate, to protect and nourish that precious seed in ourselves, and in our friends, so that we can all broaden our life choices. We are left to our own devices. If we are to breathe life into our own Jewish choice, it will be a struggle, but it can happen. I know that it is easier to sit back and fit in with everyone else. I feel that pressure every day and sometimes I try to forget and try to be a secular person. Something draws me back, and I am not alone.

All over the country tiny groups are getting together, each trying in its own way to rekindle its lights. Some people who are learned, some who are not, are exploring their Jewishness together. Many flounder at first, but feel that the struggle is worthwhile. We are confused, for there are no sure answers. But we refuse to sit by, turned off to Jewish life. We are willing to become immersed in the process of finding ourselves anew. Finding ourselves anew is our Jewish choice.

ATHLETIC CHOICES

Super Sports: Where Boys Learn to Be Men

Everyone knows what men are saying, all they talk about is sex and sports. Warren Farrell, author of *The Liberated Man*, demonstrates to us why sports are so important in the life of an all-American male and how sports and sex are related. It's not just the game that is involved, but aggression in sports is also identified with patriotism and religion. American politicians have reinforced this concept with all of their sports language as they describe U.S. foreign and domestic policy. Other political examples were Nixon's obsession with football and statements coming out of Washington like the one quoted from Marc Feigen Fasteau's book, *The Male Machine*, from the late Senator Robert F. Kennedy, "Except for war, there is nothing in American life—nothing—which trains a boy better for life than football." When we read Dr. Farrell's chapter and understand how boys learn about the aggressive, competitive, win-at-all-costs values in sports that are programming their ideas for being a real man, we can clearly see where the super sex-role stereotyping takes place—right here in super sports.

Super Sports: Where Boys Learn to Be Men*

BY WARREN FARRELL

There is nothing wrong with watching a football game. There is something suspect when a man gives lip service to "I wish I could spend more time with my wife and children" and then watches three football games in a weekend. There might be something suspect in football being held in such priority that sixty-five million people can arrange their day to allow a three-hour bloc of time for one event—the annual Super Bowl. Sixty-five million persons are between one-third and one-quarter of the American population, the very great majority of whom are men—doubtless more than half the men and boys who are old enough to watch TV in the United States.

Sixty-five million American males have chosen one activity above thousands of alternatives. This alone makes the event worthy of our attention. What are all these millions attracted to? When one adds to this the fact that this may involve persuading their wives or friends to rearrange schedules to allow the men to do this and then serve them beer and chips during the game, some attention might profitably be paid to the needs served and both the conscious and unconscious ways in which football makes its appeal to American

* Adapted from Warren Farrell, *The Liberated Man* (New York: Random House, 1974). Adapted and printed with permission of the author and publisher.

men. A systematic analysis of every part of the Super Bowl (the pregame and halftime activities, the game, and the commercials) provides some fascinating answers.

The Super Bowl's first appeal to the viewers is patriotism and power. If we follow almost any Super Bowl from beginning to end, we can see it first in the pregame activities. In the 1972 Super Bowl, alone, for example, patriotism is represented in the pregame activities by the U.S. Air Force, which uniformly, with precision and discipline, marches onto the field. They are immediately followed by four flights of Phantom jets—the Tactical Fighter Wing of the U.S. Air Force—which thunder overhead, again with precision and discipline. Power and patriotism are linked. Speed and display of force are inseparable from patriotism. The Phantom jets are just leaving the viewer's field of vision when the male announcer invokes in a deep voice (with background noise fading to silence) a plea to "remember our veterans in your prayers." Religion is now linked to power—but American power. There is no question that a God exists and that this God approves of power only as displayed by brave Americans.

The announcer's invocation needs a visual focus now that the jets are gone. The camera zooms in on the American flag. Patriotism is reinforced by music. The U.S. Air Force band plays "The Star-Spangled Banner." Feeling is running high—our jets, our Air Force, our flag, our anthem, and finally, our boys. The unquestioned power of our country is associated with the discipline and uniformity of every Air Force jet and Air Force marching-band member. No deviance is tolerated in this display. Freedom of choice seems to be every man choosing short hair, since there was no man in the pregame activities without it. The power of "The Star-Spangled Banner" reached enormous heights, but it is followed by a final call to patriotism—the U.S. Marine Corps's silent drill team marching in quiet but precise step. This is the silence following the climax. Now the American male may watch the game.

Football, like war, is a scientific and brutal game; even the vocabulary of football is similar to that of war. A "bomb" is something thrown that destroys the opposite side. To bomb effectively is to "score." There is always an us and a them. There are commands to take the offensive and to prepare one's defenses. Both football and war feature spying and scouting, and special units for extra degrees of violence. (When the vocabulary is not interchangeable with that of war, it is with that of sex: "getting into the hole," "thrusting," and the announcer's admiration for each man successful at "deep penetration.")

The special team employed during every kickoff or punt is called the suicide squad. The comparison to war is made by Rich Saul, a lineman for the Los Angeles Rams who is notorious for his play on suicide squads. "If you compare football to war, then the special teams are the marines or the infantry. We're the first ones to get into the game, we initiate the hitting, we determine where the battle is going to be fought and on whose grounds." Saul, who says he enjoys his job, "slams into ball carriers with such intensity that he mangled five steel face masks on the front of his helmet." John Bramlett, a thirty-year-old veteran, says, "I think about hurting the other person because every time you get kicked senseless, you can count on knocking two or three other people senseless. That's a pretty good feeling." Fans made a legend out of Gil Mains of Detroit almost ten years ago. His fame was based on his willingness to launch himself feet first at the heart of an offensive wedge (a group of about four especially tough and quick men who block for the ball carrier). His attacking position is commonly called a "head-hunter" (his primary aim is to get the ball carrier's head). On the special teams the injury rate is eight times greater than for any other position.

The dependence on approval is so great that players continue to play with injuries no matter how painful they are. The men entering the suicide squads are tough men who use their strength as a way of compensating for their insecurity about making it on the club in any other way. These men are "mostly tough rookies and second-year men" who "realize that their survival on the club—and the road to a starting job— is directly related to their ferocity and fearlessness."

On the field a series of rituals are taking place that are designated to reinforce and provoke the utmost aggressiveness of which each man is capable. The pep talk is one ritual. The boy is manipulated by a number of reinforcing loyalties—the loyalty to his school, the coach, his team and team pride, and his own personal pride. In the game itself the loyalty to family and neighbors is added. Prior to the game the team captain yells, "O.K., let's go get them!" and the team screams, "Yeah!" repeatedly. A third ritual, described by Dave Meggyesy, formerly of the St. Louis Cardinals, as part of his high-school team's preparation, is a special church service by a minister (a former college athlete), who gives an inspirational talk. Almost every type of tactic is permitted when the boys go all out for victory. The side with which one identifies is seen as all good and the other as all bad.

If the effect of professional football is not clear by the end of the first half of the game, it becomes clear at halftime. The first event is the introduction of young male children who will competitively vie with each other for honors such as the best passer. Seven-year-old boys test their strength before sixty-five million people, and the young boy at home sees already that he is not quite the man some of his peers are. Furthermore, the other person with whom he identifies is sitting an arm's length away, glued to the TV set. Both the football game and the presence of his father increase the boy's sense of identity with both, but somehow he often feels he is not yet worthy of being a part of what is on the field or deserving of full attention of his father. If the father is a rabid football fan and the boy a fair-to-middling athlete, the father's presence reinforces the son's need to identify without enabling him to get the feedback to fulfill that need. There is no consistent transmittal of that warm feeling which tells the son he is accepted. Such a boy will either try to prove himself on various playing fields or will live vicariously through men who can.

No sooner do the boys clear off the field than women (called "girls") come onto the field. They are scantily clad, swinging their hips in unison, with outfits cut to reveal their buttocks and bosoms. As the cameras zero in on the former, their legs slowly withdraw in a coy but obvious "see if you can get me."

The "girls" are not only selling the importance of slim, sexually coy bodies, they are selling the importance of white bodies (not a brown or black face was among the hundreds onto which the camera focused). But the sexism of selling bodies and the racism of uniform whiteness was not enough. These women were used to sell American patriotism. The scanty outfits were red, white, and blue "Aunt Sam" outfits, and in case the point was missed, each girl had a plastic American flag molded into an umbrella. As the distorted flag umbrellas were opened and closed, the announcer explained the theme—"remembering the birth of America."

While sex is selling patriotism on the ground, power is used to sell it from the air. U.S. Air Force jets fly overhead, dropping dozens of American flags amid a cloud of smoke and a huge burst of firecrackers. The flags are distorted so as to fit into a parachute. The camera now returns us to the ground and the "girls," where we witness hundreds of plastic flags laid on the ground and being danced around by the "girls."

The next group of ladies appear in frilly red tights cut similarly to those of the last group. These women sing "Hello, Dolly" and literally lie around in a circle on the field and spread their legs, lift them up, and spread them again. Carol Channing also sings "Hello, Dolly." Suddenly dozens of dollies appear—it's the women in red tights who now promenade off the field by passing the men. The camera zooms in to pick up the eye contact between the men and the women, the essence of the halftime game. The proper distance is always maintained. The men have made their eyes while maintaining their stiff all-male ensemble, and the women have made their appeal without physically being "had." The half time ends. The women who are on the field because of their bodies leave the field to make way for the men who will come on the field because of their bodies.

The viewer has now come through half a game and the halftime. On the conscious level the man's power has been supported by his identification with the football players and his fantasizing an "I'd like to get her" relationship with one of "the girls" the camera brought into his living room. In fact, during a Cornell at Dartmouth game, the ABC cameras picked out individual women in the stands and rated them. The evaluations (by males) were literally placed on the TV screen as "not too bad," "terrific," and other more condescending phrases. An ABC-TV spokesman indicated in a telephone interview that this was used on four broadcasts. It was not an isolated incident and the pressure brought to bear on the network was obviously not great enough to make it discontinue its use (the spokesman said he "did not remember any reactions to this").

The armchair viewers of the Super Bowl meanwhile have been treated to a spectacle which the crowd at the stadium has missed—the commercials. The theme of all but two of the commercials was muscle, strength, power, and speed (no different from the football game). The first of two exceptions featured five women in sexy outfits attempting to gain the favor of one man by being chosen to serve him a Dutch Master cigar. The man, literally on a throne, acts unaffected and coolly discriminating as the five women move their bodies carelessly toward him in repeated attempts to be recognized. The smoke from the cigars creates a fantasy atmosphere of clouds as the commercial ends, along with the fantasy of millions of men.

The second exception is the only advertisement that deals even remotely with emotions or with a father's

Warren Farrell

relationship with his children. Four-fifths of the commercial is an incredibly good portrait of a close and warm father-child relationship. Then the father is told he might die. It is implied that if he loves his children he will buy insurance. His love has been exploited and twisted into fear for the purpose of selling him insurance. Now the father has a way of showing his love for his children: he can spend money. He alone is responsible for their support, if he's living or if he's dead.

A beer advertisement first prepares us for the introduction of the beer. We see a rowing team of all men. The camera focuses on their muscles—the strength and power of the men become clear, but they all take directions perfectly from their leader. The importance of strict obedience is coupled with victory, and victory coupled with being a man. The beer is introduced as the well-earned reward, with the concluding comment, "It's sort of good to be with men who won't settle for second best."

The razor-blade ad follows a similar pattern. The blades are tungsten, but they are not introduced until they are associated with a powerful steelworker drilling through tough tungsten steel. His shirt sleeve is cut short (and ragged) to reveal his muscles. Sparks bounce off his helmet. He balances himself above the city drilling the steel that makes the city (a far cry from "softer hands with Dove"). Now the tungsten blades can be introduced. They are blades "as tough as steel, for men with tough beards."

The marketing researchers know where it's at. Most of the ads were car ads—cars with "wire-grip tires" (not "pretty whitewalls"), with tremendous speed, and generally from the sports-car lines of whatever company is advertising. Men want adventure, freedom, a feeling of power, strength, and status. They think that they are untouchable and unemotional, and are unaware that they are totally psychologically dependent on an authority figure. But marketing researchers reinforce this dilemma even more adeptly during the football season. The new theme is selling products through the *fear* of becoming *effeminate* (as opposed to the *aspiration* of becoming *masculine*). Perhaps a New York Life Insurance ad illustrates this best:

A bespectacled, effeminately portrayed man in a white shirt and tie is pictured in the middle of a football field surrounded by eleven muscular football players—in uniform. By mistake the ball lands in his hands. By mistake he trips his way toward the goal line, stumbling haphazardly past each player. His wife is shouting from the stands, "Come on, Hubby, make it for the mortgage"; his daughter is shouting, "Come on, Daddy, make it for my college education"; the dog is almost pissing on the bleachers at the shock of seeing his effeminate master reaching his goal. Daddy trips and stumbles past another, then still another astonished "real" football player. With a look of happy bewilderment he finds he has made a touchdown. His wife, daughter, and dog run from the stands—kissing, hugging, and praising their hero. Daddy is stunned.

The male voice-over announcer is not stunned. He has the answer: Daddy is being protected by New York Life Insurance Company to make it to his goals. New York Life Insurance Company has spent the entire commercial showing millions of men a symbol of a daddy who fears not being able to make it to his goal of bringing the bacon (represented by the football) home (represented by the goal line); who fears he is surrounded by barriers of invulnerable managers and executives (represented by the football players) through whom he will only be able to "muddle through" at best; *who thinks he is being supported by the cheers of his family from the stands, but somehow recognizes that every cheer is a pressure*. Every cheer is a pressure to "make it"; it is the woman saying, "I don't have any control over the mortgage. I have to cheer you on to do something about it. I have to make a man of you." It is the daughter saying, "I don't have any control over my college education, but I can cheer, 'I love you, Daddy, if only you'll make it.'" In his own way the dog cheers too, and in his own way the dog is still another pressure.

In a world where men's cheerleaders are men's pressures, who supports the man? New York Life Insurance is there in case we can't make it. It, too, is a pressure which twists us into understanding our burden just enough to seek the protection of having it shared with our partner. The motto of New York Life is "We guarantee tomorrow today." New York Life understands. It does not run these ads during soap operas. *Its* phallic symbols are rising.

The game draws to a close. The winning coach is Tom Landry, "the man they say is unemotional." The winning team is the Dallas Cowboys, "the team they say is unemotional." But the victory is tremendous, a clear-cut triumph: 24 to 3. The cameras pick the victorious coach out of the crowd. He barely cracks a smile. The time for emotions is certainly here, a few of the football players do express happiness, but the game ends on a note of patriotism, not emotionalism. The National Football League champions are repeatedly referred to as the world champions. There are no boundaries to male power and no limits on male fantasies—except emotional limits.

SUPER SPORTS

If this relationship between masculinity, sexism, patriotism, and violence stopped with professional football, there would be enough need for concern. However, the relationship can be seen in almost every sport. With some exceptions the more violent the game or match, the larger the crowd it draws. The emphasis on violence is not unrelated to what is making ice hockey grow. The television advertisements for ice hockey stress quite clearly the blocking, hard-hitting, and violent aspects of the sport. Soccer is the most popular sport in the world but has barely caught on in the United States. Persons who have lived in the United States and other countries observe that, even when soccer is played here, the emphasis on body contact is great—a phenomenon peculiar to this country.

On almost all the levels on which sports are played, sexism is a fundamental part. What high-school basketball game is without cheerleaders to support the men's efforts? In many schools cheerleaders even support grammar school teams, and for a girl, "making it" as a cheerleader is as important a step in her view of herself as feminine as making the team is in the man's view of himself as masculine. Cheerleaders are still essential in college football, high-school football, and college basketball. The *New York Post* captured the identity problem of the woman cheerleader most graphically in a picture of a crying cheerleader slumped on the floor after Fordham lost in the 1972 NIT play-offs. Obviously, the more the cheerleader supports, the more pressure is on the man to perform.

The woman, of course, cannot usually influence the outcome of the game by *playing in it*. If participation of both sexes is permitted, the spotlight still shines on the masculine contest.

SUPER-JOCK

While the amount of attention the girl receives is minimal, the attention the boy receives really places considerable pressure on him. Every time the announcer broadcasts the achievement of another boy, the pressure for him to perform or score increases. With the lights flashing and his father shouting, the boy has much more than his self-evaluation at stake. The rewards after the game are sweet for the achiever but bitter for the nonachiever. There is no overt punishment, just the punishment of being left out. The boy who did not even make the team is relegated to being completely "left out."

"Well," most fathers will reply, "this is all in fun, and besides, any real boy learns to take the ups with the downs." In some ways boys do—they soon learn to take it by learning to become well-defended. Sarcasms, witticisms, and put-downs become the common

mode of communication with their "friends." Underneath, though, boys do not learn to "take it." Few boys
escape adolescence without an ego so fragile that only
a woman who will spend her life supporting it can be
tolerated. Secretly they all yearn to be a super-jock.

The physical striver, as we have seen, is in fact quite
insecure. The surface toughness, independence, and
masculinity of the football player often mask his need
to be dominated. Meggyesy discusses the many ways
in which the "father-son relationship is football's
cornerstone." He describes how players look up to,
respect, and desperately want approval from the coach.
The coach who is respected is tough; he never shows
feelings. The players need to be dominated and controlled by such a strong man.

A coach will chastise a player by saying he looks
"almost feminine" on the field. Meggyesy points out
that "this sort of attack on a player's manhood is a
coach's doomsday weapon. And it works, for the
players have wrapped up their identity in their masculinity, which is eternally precarious, for it not only
depends on not exhibiting fear of any kind on the
playing field, but is something that can be given and
withdrawn by a coach at his pleasure." Not only does
the coach exploit a fragile masculinity, but he also ex-
ploits a firm fear of femininity.

With women, though, the athletes are free to do as
they like. In high school, players are encouraged to behave in a rough, aggressive manner both on and off the
field. Players are even bailed out of jail and gotten out
of other trouble by the coaches. The coaches view these
activities as "sowing wild oats."

Both coaches and players consider it "healthy and
manly" to get drunk, lay a girl, and "maybe even rough
her up a bit." Meggyesy explains that to the football
player "wives are virginal creatures keeping the home
and children; other women are meat on the rack."
However, a lasting relationship is viewed with sus-
picion and even considered immoral. There is a lot of
bragging about sex among football players, but when a

woman is around, their self-doubt and nervousness shows.

The insecure man is one who often gets trapped into proving himself a man. *It is through this need that society can manipulate him.* He is especially subject to being manipulated into committing violent acts by the approval of the football coach or the army general, the gang leader, other peers, their parents, the public, or fans. The one thing he cannot do is defend what he believes in against the clamor of the crowd. It also may be doubted that he really knows what he believes in.

Discovery Through Sports

If it's true that a student can learn best about competition, leadership, cooperation, and friendship through sports, then doesn't it make sense to have everyone in on it? Dr. Shepard, professor emeritus of Denison University, and first chairperson who integrated the men's and women's departments of physical education, writes about sports as a way of discovering more about yourself. Sports is a way to learn about competitiveness, stress, and risk taking, fascination of the unknown, and sports as belonging as a member of a team. There is a total involvement in sports that takes you out of an ordinary, everyday life situation, and that exhilaration can belong to all of you—through sports.

Discovery Through Sports

BY NATALIE M. SHEPARD

Members of the human race have engaged in competitive sports since the dawn of time, but the world of super sports, as we know them today, is a possession of the few. Television with its marvelous coverage of sports events has brought the super athlete into every home as a model for emulation and example.

But super sport is not for everyone. What if you can't make it in sports? Usually you either quit completely, with a lifelong disdain for sports and a consequent loss of its many pleasures for the rest of your life; or you keep trying, in a losing battle, accepting standards set by your parents or peers that have nothing to do with your *own talents* or interests.

Athletes and their promoters have eagerly sought the supportive role of the nonathlete as the super spectator. Watch and applaud. Accept and idealize. Praise and support. But a new way to be part of the action and a new understanding of the values of sport are long overdue. Athletics and sports are *not* the same thing. Although athletics may be included in sport, sport includes more than athletics. And while athletics are not for everyone, and team membership does exclude many, sports has a range and variety that permits *everyone* to get into the action.

WHAT IS SPORT?

Sport is many things to many people. For some it is the same as games and means any activity from children's run and tag to the recreational pursuits of adults. For others it means only the "major" sports of high school, college, and the pro circuits. But what about waterskiing, skydiving, jogging, and backpacking? Are these sports, too? What about skiing and snow shoeing, swimming, fishing, boating, tennis, and golf? Does the activity need to demand strenuous physical exertion? Must it be competitive, or can it include fishing, camping, and watching TV? Are you a sportsperson only if you participate, or can you be a watcher and belong too?

In the first place, sport includes physical exertion and, in the main, sports mean activity. Whether we watch or play, strenuous physical effort is involved in every game situation.

In the second place, sport is a clearly defined task set apart from the ordinary. A code is developed to which all agree. This code establishes the rules and one enters the "set-apartness" voluntarily. If you don't agree to the game, you don't play. For example: Here is the equipment: one ball, one pair of skis, one tennis racket, one club; here is the playing area: one field, one tennis court, one mountain, or one pool; here are the rules and regulations, the prescription of what one may or may not do and how one shall behave. Here, too, is the goal or purpose: what shall be attempted and under what circumstances and restrictions. The essential question, the challenge, the impelling fascination: how well can the person do what is prescribed? Within these limitations how well can one perform?

In the third place, the sports world contrasts sharply with the ordinary, everyday world. In sport there is the freedom of choice. Much of life requires jobs that are necessary and required, but the sports choices are voluntary and therefore much more fun. Furthermore, life is so complex that we always have to divide our attention. But the sports world presents a single job on which all of one's being can be focused. It *feels good* to focus one's whole self in this fashion, to get free from being pulled in a dozen different directions. For the short period of the game experience, there is no fragmentation, no divided attention. One can experience being a whole person. Human beings *need* to exercise their bodies, need to use their human capacities for a movement and energy expenditure, need to experience the exhilaration of complete wholeness, of being all of one piece!

WHY PLAY SPORTS?

I suspect that all the reasons that can be brought forward can be placed under the single heading of fun. *Look* magazine once ran an article under the title "Ordeal of Fun" and described with beautiful inclusion the many facets of the world of recreation and sports, the beauty, the pain, the challenge, the adventure, the risk taking, the rustic pleasure of a rural setting, the whole lovely gamut of things people do because it is *fun*. Why will you play sports? Why the delight in these activities that run so close to madness in their compelling urge to perform? Self-knowledge, competitiveness, stress and risk taking, fascination of the unknown, health and fitness, and belonging are some of the reasons.

SELF-KNOWLEDGE

Surely part of the reason for living is to know oneself. How you achieve this self-knowing has been the subject of endless speculation, meditation, and thoughtful analysis by the prophets of all time. All of life's experiences contribute to it, and so, too, the world of sports has much to offer. Some would say that the game situation presents *unique* opportunities, a special laboratory, because the whole self is involved. Your complete attention and enthusiasm are focused on one single task and thus the sport experience is integrating.

If you wish to know yourself, or another, put yourself in a position of stress. There is anxiety, fear, challenge, a chancy situation where failure is possible and very real, where success is possible and very real, and where the result depends entirely on a situation where *your* efforts, your skill, your competence make the differences. Try bicycling down a steep gravel road where acceleration takes you ever faster, and a skid means a fall and physical injury. But a skillful passage means exhilaration, no skid or fall, but the thrill of your own achievement and new confidence in yourself. As for the "other," or for yourself, what is revealed in the experience of your relationships in this ride? Is there bullying, ridicule, impatience, unkindness if there is injury? Is there openness, caring, kindness? Is there pleasure in the success of the other person, patience with failure, generosity in the difference exposed by the achievement? Does not even a game of cards make some of the same revelations? Greed, intent to win at all costs, cheating when the chance arises, or generosity, fairness, helpfulness for the one who is just learning? The list of meanings in these game and sport situations is as endless as the gamut of human emotions, and as revealing.

STRESS AND RISK TAKING

Sports provide varying opportunities for us to know ourselves in moments of stress—certain sports more than others, although almost any provide some of this element. The element of risk taking and of stress seeking is illustrated in any sport where physical exertion is required. You train, you condition yourself to peak physical health so that you can give yourself with

abandon, making the difficult look easy, with perfection
as the only goal and also the only safety. The thrill
is in the risk taking. You sky-dive, spelunk, drive racing
cars, rock-climb, stunt-fly, ski-sail, skin- and scuba-
dive, high-jump and pole-vault, swim and race to exhaustion. You do these things because it *feels good* to
expend yourself completely, to use your human abilities
to the utmost.

Among other sports, the Outward Bound programs
of three-week sessions are designed precisely for the
experience of self-knowing under stress. Gradually
skills are developed and the body conditioned to the
peak of your physical capacities. In addition, living together during the sessions, you seek new understandings
of reliance on others and new experiences of confidence
in yourself. Putting it all together, the final purpose of
all the preparation is found when tests of risk taking
and adventure are designed to reveal the self-knowledge
of your own outer limits. The whole purpose is to test
the limits of your endurance—not another's but your
own. When you are there, the person you wrestle with
is yourself, your own fear, your own courage, your own
strength. Every personal resource is utilized until you
stand naked before your own self-knowing.

In the moments of stress, when all excuses or pre-
tenses are stripped away, stress and risk taking in the
sports world reveal you to yourself. You perform on
the uneven parallels risking everything in the speed and
disciplined abandon of your flying dismount, or you
leap higher than ever before on your hurdle for the
exacting forward one-and-a-half somersault with full
twist from the diving board. You catch the ball, or you
fumble it; you have the staying power when the climb
is steep, or you haven't. It is your skill, your training,
your courage that make the difference. This is the
reason the stress and risk taking are thrilling; the pride
in your accomplishment is against real, not phony, odds.

Our society does not value nonproductive activities.
When the person has climbed the mountain and reached
the peak, when the vault or the dive is made with the

breathtaking beauty of the human form in motion and the action is completed—what is there to show for it? People are sometimes killed in their sports adventures and society mourns their passing as a pitiful waste of human potential. *Why* do people risk their lives in these seemingly senseless tasks? The answer lies in the self-knowingness. The explanation is in the *process* of the whole wonderful experience, rather than in the "nothing to show for it," nonproduct aspect at the completion of the action. To *do* it is enough. To be involved, to focus, and the completeness of expending oneself are an altogether experience. An integrated action, one that leads to the person's self-knowing and the recognition of his or her personhood.

FASCINATION OF THE UNKNOWN

All sports contain the unknown. It is part of risk taking, part of the chanciness of the outcome of a contest, part of the stress and yet-to-be-revealed ability or nonability to sustain effort in the circumstance. The fascination of the unknown is the self-propelling ingredient in any game situation. Who will win, who will lose, who has what it takes, who is not ready for the contest?

Other aspects of the unknown are superbly inherent in an environment that is out of the ordinary; that is, in the world of water and aquatics, or the world of air and skydiving, or the world of the wilderness in contrast to our cities and towns. Some sports are at home in these environments.

Consider the world of aquatics and the exploration of the unknown in its environmental qualities. To learn to swim and dive, to understand the nature of this medium, to water-ski and boat, to sail and white-water canoe—there are excitement and thrill here. What fascination as its wonders are revealed! What freedom for adventure and for challenge lies in the achievement of basic skills in this water medium!

In the same way consider the way of the wilderness.

It is not for all, but for those who train themselves in the skills needed to enjoy it, it is a lifetime of pleasure and satisfaction. Adventure and challenge in ever-widening horizons beckon the explorer. The skills to enjoy it are too numerous to list but must include something of camping and survival activities, hiking and backpacking, mountaineering, nature study, and ecology. So many facets of beauty are filled with the fascination of the unknown. Here is meaning and here reasons for being in the world of sports that uses the wilderness for its playing fields.

HEALH AND FITNESS

Until we are deprived of good health, who ever heard of doing things that we know are good for us just because we should? Health and physical fitness can and must be achieved, not as a goal, but as a by-product. As you play the sports you want to play, fitness and well-being come naturally through your activities. You keep in condition, you watch your weight and your nutrition, you exercise and condition your body *so that you can participate well*. Your purpose is to play the game, to perform with excellence, to be able to go the limit and not tire—to play, and play, and play again.

It's a little bit like happiness, or laughter, this being healthy and fit. If one seeks it for its own sake, it eludes one. Happiness and laughter cannot be forced. They come as a by-product of living with joy and abandon and giving of oneself, of loving and caring and good friendships. Fitness and good health come in this way. The by-product of exciting, challenging, thoroughly productive good sports participation *is* glowing good health and fitness.

BELONGING

Along with self-knowledge, the sports world offers the precious qualities of friendship and the chance to earn the right to belong. In no other situation is this human need more readily fulfilled. One enters the sports world by choice, a voluntary act, and in it joins with others in a world completely their own. This world is divorced from the ordinary, set apart with its own rules and prescription so that under no other circumstances are the requirements to belong more clearly defined. Do this task and do it well. If you play you are "in," you belong. Sport is color-blind and money-blind. You cannot buy your way in. You belong because you are playing. You can give laughter and make us all happier; you can encourage when we need that extra push. You lead and we follow because you can help us to win. Our battle may be against another team, against a machine or a mountain, or against ourselves. In spelunking you give us courage against the fear of the dark and the exploration of the unknown. In white-water canoeing you give us strength when we need one more paddle push against exhaustion and a turn over. In skiing you go first and show us that it can be done. In basketball, when there are just two minutes left, you have the courage and strength to stage a rally that gets us by with one point with no minutes to spare.

And when the exhilaration and the excitement of the game are over, we leave the sports world for the everyday world. We go back to our cultural divisions and our differences, but whenever we meet or remember, we "belong" together for that one thing we did, that one period we played together. We talk about it ceaselessly, we recall point by point, incident and moment by moment the fun we had, the failure when we didn't quite make it, the joy of achievement when we did. Belonging is one of the most fundamental of human needs, and the sports world offers each person the opportunity to join. You bring yourself and offer what you have.

MORE READING ABOUT SPORTS

Leonard, George. *The Ultimate Athlete.* New York: The Viking Press, 1974.

Lipsyte, Robert. *Sportsworld: An American Dream World.* New York: Quadrangle, 1975.

Meggyesy, Dave. *Out of Their League.* New York: Warner Paperback Library, 1971.

Shaw, Gary. *Meat on the Hoof.* New York: Dell, 1973.

EDUCATIONAL CHOICES

In High School

Study Is for Learning

Having the answers in class and being cool about learning are part of the masculine mystique. Boys and young men often act as if they are supposed to know their homework and subjects so well that they don't have to study. They compete with each other for the *least* amount of time and effort they appear to put in on the books. This kind of competition goes on as if good study habits were a put-down for young men. Don't believe it! All students need good study habits. You will want efficient study habits so that you will have more time of your own, whether your time is for more study, or sports, or earning money, or playing in a music group.

Here is some help with developing good study habits. First, in order for you to make improvements, you must define study as your work. And as work that counts—give it top priority. Studying isn't just something everyone who goes to school has to do. it's your job, your way to discover and learn about the world. Next, as soon as studying becomes more to you than "homework," you will see it as a worthwhile skill. Not because the school says so, but because it's your way of making your contribution to understanding the world.

Study Is for Learning

BY JOYCE SLAYTON MITCHELL

Studying is work, *your* work. It is hard work and it must be done alone. Your mother and father have their daily work, long-term jobs, routine jobs, things they like and things they don't like about their work. You can expect the same from your schoolwork. Studying isn't natural. It may look as though it's easy for others to study because they are some kind of "study creature"—but study is learned behavior and everyone who is a good worker has learned it. The sooner you realize that studying is not something extra, the sooner you realize the need for the skill. Hopefully you will then begin to get the enjoyment out of the real reason for study . . . learning.

Many teachers, educators, and parents promote the idea that the classroom is the heart of learning. Studying then becomes doing something for the teacher or cramming for tests and examinations. In fact, the classroom situation is only your guide for what to study, your evaluation of how you do, your suggestions for new ways to look at materials such as tests, related readings, papers, and projects about the particular subject.

In order to look at studying as something that has to do with *you*, you should understand that studying is for learning. And learning is what high school is all about. It is learning what you can do academically, what you can understand, how you can relate to new materials, what you can think about.

In order to get anything out of studying, you must define it in such a way that it is important to you. You must set it up in your mind so that it counts. It has to have a top priority if it is going to work. If you can possibly define your study time as your work, and that you must work nights, it will help. There is no question about the difficulty of the hour, especially if your parents are home from their work and watching TV or playing bridge or having late cocktails and dinner while you work—but your schedule is different. You have sports, and clubs, and time off for activities after school while your parents or most adults are still on their jobs. At any rate, it won't come out fair or equal with adults because high-school students who study on a regular, responsible basis *do* work more than adults who have a nine-to-five job. Your work schedule compares more readily with professional people in teaching, research, law, and medicine, or with business executives who work all hours. There is no doubt that a high-school student who studies three hours a night works more than the forty-hour week! And three hours a night is about average for an A or B student with five academic subjects in a competitive high school.

As you work out your study schedule and find what you can do in terms of working alone, at the library, or with homework assignments, you will be learning what you can do in college, what you can do in your career after college. All your high-school experiences are teaching you about your abilities and your interests. Studying is a key place for you to learn about your self-starting ability, your motivation, your persistence, your follow-through, and your ability to stick with a problem. These traits will build. You will learn all kinds of things that you can do as well as all kinds of things you definitely cannot do because of your lack of good study skills.

Your ability to study will be better by your third year in high school than it was in your first year. Self-discipline is a growing ability. Good study skills grow slowly. It takes time to learn to use your mind efficiently to understand all kinds of subjects, to memorize facts, to grasp new ideas, and to see relationships between the subjects you study and you and the world. If there is no way for you and study skills, then you should know that, for you, there is no way for you and college, or at least a liberal arts or competitive college.

HOW CAN YOU STUDY TO LEARN?

Many things will help you to study. Good teachers and interested parents who encourage you and work with you as you develop your study skills are the most help. But good teachers and interested parents are hard to find, and lucky is the student who has either! If you ask for help with your studying, from your homeroom teacher or your guidance counselor or one of the administrators, you should be able to find someone who will encourage you so that your work will be something you look forward to.

If your family is working against you with distracting offers of other things to do and with noise in the house, you may be able to go to the local library, or to study as much as possible in school or after school, in place of sports or music or clubs. Some students do all their studying before they go home because they know that conditions at home just don't work for study. These students get their work done right after school, in place of extracurricular school activities. They spend their time off with their families at night.

There are many books written about how to study, or chapters in books about study, and lists of dos and don'ts for studying. They explain that you need a nice warm comfortable room, good light, no radio or TV, no wandering thoughts, plenty of paper and supplies, and time. And, of course, the proper assignment. Many of you know that all of these physical things can be in place, but after the first two or three tries of a new school year, it just doesn't work. Potato chips are added, the radio is on low, the phone rings for just one call, or a TV special is on from eight to nine that night. In other words—planning the study time and place and being there aren't the same as doing the work.

DOING THE WORK

Plan the amount of time you are going to work or study. Don't let yourself get away with reasons to change the time after you have made just one phone call or visit with a sister or brother. Figure out exactly what you want to accomplish with a specific goal for each subject. So many problems in mathematics, so many pages of history to outline, so many words to memorize in French. If you have one hour for each subject, and you start with mathematics, when the hour is up and you are only half finished, go on to the next subject. Don't use all three hours on the mathematics! Either you didn't understand the assignment, or it is too hard and the whole class won't get it either, or you aren't going to make it in math. At least not tomorrow. Go on to the French for the next hour, and to the history for the third hour. If there is time left over after working on all three subjects, go back to the mathematics. *Organize* your time. Experience will help you with this, and your time will be used more effectively when you stick to alloted times. You have heard that people with the most to do get the most done—it's the same principle. If you have all day to clean the garage, you can take all day to do it, or if you have to clean it in one hour in order to go to the game, you can do it in the one hour. Don't let yourself spend all night or all day on one assignment.

Plan which assignments you will do in what order. Some students start with their favorite, in order to get going faster, and others begin with their least favorite, in order to get it over with so that they aren't too tired at the end with the worst subject left to do. After an hour at your desk, take a planned five- or ten-minute break. Get a snack or talk to someone or turn on the music and walk around and stretch.

Don't wait until a subject interests you before you plan to do the homework! Until you learn enough about it, it couldn't possibly interest you. You have to do your social studies or Latin or geometry assignments whether you like them or not. And good students *become* interested in subjects because of study.

Even though the subject doesn't interest you, the best study takes place when you know why you are studying, you care about what you are studying, and you are certain you can actually do the work. Try to understand the work for its own sake. Learn how *you* do in the subject, not how much you have to do in order to please a teacher or get a particular grade.

Memorizing

No matter how modern the school you attend, or no matter what the latest fashion in learning is, you can't get very far without memorizing. There is vocabulary to memorize, scientific formulas, events, names of people, historical periods as well as specific dates of events to learn. You can't write a good examination without specifically memorizing information.

There are some helpful tips for memorizing. The most obvious is that the more you understand about what you are trying to memorize, the easier it is to remember. Many students have difficulty memorizing simply because they haven't taken the time to understand the concept in the first place.

Concentrate on what you are trying to memorize and use as many senses as possible to learn. Read the material aloud so that you can hear as well as see it. Don't try spending long hours at a time, beyond your efficiency for memorizing. Fifteen- to twenty-minute sessions with other homework in between the memorizing sessions are the most effective way to memorize for most students. Going over the memorization just before class is always a help—not to learn but to recall the poem or facts or vocabulary.

Testing

You will periodically be tested on the materials you covered during the school term. If you really do understand the subject, you will be able to use your study time for review for these tests and examinations. If you have worked just enough to get by for your daily assignments, and you called that studying, then all of your review time has to be spent cramming or learning the material for the first time! Cramming can work for one or two subjects, but it will never work for four or five strong subjects if you plan to do *well* in them.

A bright student *can* attend classes, cram, and learn enough to pass a test in all of his courses; but if academic work is something you want to develop and grow into a meaningful activity in your life, then studying *must* take a priority right *now*.

Learning

Actually, the word "learning" or "understanding" has more to do with you than the word "homework" (which sounds as though it's for the teacher) or the word "studying" (which sounds as though working for the sake of the work). If you think of studying as learning or understanding new things and people and concepts or discovery, it may help. You want all the help you can get for this skill of studying to learn on your own, as it has to be.

WHERE CAN YOU GO FOR MORE HELP IN LEARNING?

There is no substitute for the teacher of a course to help you to learn. Different subjects must be studied differently; to go to the mathematics or foreign language or history teacher is by far the most relevant help you can get. Don't be afraid to ask them how to study to learn their particular subject. Most teachers will be pleased with your interest, since usually teachers feel that the last interest students have is studying to learn. For this very reason many teachers don't teach you about studying. Don't wait until you are in a crisis to ask for help, especially if it's a new subject for you and you aren't getting the understanding of it that you expected to have. Go to the teacher while it concerns *you*—not when your lack of understanding also concerns your teacher, your parents, and your counselor. By that time you are into reasons removed from you and learning.

Educational Decisions

The sooner you take your work seriously (learning) the sooner it will become very meaningful and worthwhile for you to be spending those three hours every night at it. You will be surprised at how interesting your work can be! Remember it is *you* who are learning and understanding. You are becoming a person who needs to know as much about your learning ability as you can know in order to make those curriculum, educational, vocational, and career decisions that you will have to make.

Read to Learn

You can learn how to be a good reader, how to improve your reading, what to read, the importance of a good vocabulary, and how to use the reading list in this chapter.

You read to learn your reactions to things that sound like you and that don't sound like you. You can learn where you stand in the range of other people's experiences on issues that concern you.

If your life includes being a serious student, then reading is the critical skill for you to possess—and to enjoy!

Read to Learn

BY JOYCE SLAYTON MITCHELL

The best readers read a lot! The more you read, the better you read; the better you read, the more you understand. Schoolwork and learning revolve around reading. It is the fundamental skill needed for you to become an educated person. If you plan to continue beyond high school, reading will be the crucial skill for you to possess—and *enjoy*.

Are you a good reader? Here are some things that will help you to know:

> A good reader reads easily and fast.
> He understands what he reads.
> He remembers what he reads.
> He reads groups of words—thought patterns—rather than word by word.
> He reads at different speeds depending on the purpose of his reading (test, pleasure, contrasting ideas).
> He has a good vocabulary and continually adds to it.
> He reads critically and questions the source and purpose of the author. He doesn't believe "everything in print."
> He reads all kinds and types of materials and books.
> He loves to read.

Everyone can improve his reading. Most of us don't read as fast as we could because we have been taught to read slowly in order to get all the facts. Many students don't see any reason for reading any faster.

Nevertheless, you will get more and more reading assigned to you as you continue in school, you will get more interested in related books, and you will hear about books you wish you had time to read that aren't related to anything you are studying in school. The faster you can read, the faster you can finish your required reading and read something of your choice.

A good reader knows which materials to read fast and which will take more time. All reading shouldn't be at the same speed. If you are taking notes to write a term paper, or memorizing dates or formulas as you read—these things must be read more slowly. If you are reading the newspaper, a novel, or an essay, you can read much faster and learn to skim in order to get the main point. A good reader has learned to decide what speed is necessary for the job.

HOW TO IMPROVE YOUR READING

When you start reading, know what you are reading for: the main idea, particular facts, pleasure, to compare the same subject with another author, or for ideas to write something of your own. Learn to look at the reading material: its length, the names of the chapters, the headings used in the text, and the summary. This information will give you an idea of the style and organization of the author. Most articles can be understood by reading the opening sentence to find the problem the author is going to write about and the final paragraphs of his or her summary. Many things you select to read won't be what you had thought they were, so don't read them through after you know they are not what you needed. Learn to browse, to explore; try a book, and if you decide it isn't right, then choose another one.

Push yourself to read faster, practice some rapid reading every day. Use a ruler and move it down the page at a regular rate and see how fast you can cover the page, trying not to move your head or saying the words in your throat. All the physical motions with head and eyes and voice slow your reading rate. Look at as many words at a time as you can, and learn to give your full attention to what you are reading. Don't use your brain power to block out a radio program when you can use it to concentrate on your reading and your understanding of what you read. Really try to develop a fast and good reading style.

DEVELOPING YOUR VOCABULARY

Developing your vocabulary is a by-product of reading. You can't learn or understand any more than your understanding and knowledge of words will permit. The larger your vocabulary, the more you can understand what you read, and the more ideas you will have to express yourself in writing and speaking. Vocabulary is the most significant measurement of a student's intelligence and ability to do well in school. If schools had to use only one test to predict success in school, they would use the test that measures vocabulary.

You may have heard about many methods to improve your vocabulary such as special courses, books, special schooling, and lists to memorize which increase your vocabulary in a week or a month. But the most logical and reliable way to build your vocabulary is by working with words as you read. This doesn't mean to interrupt your reading to look up every word you don't understand as you go along. If you can guess at the meaning of a word through context, make a note of it and look it up when you have finished. Nothing could make reading more uninteresting than to stop with every few paragraphs to use a dictionary.

However, figuring out the general meaning of words as you go along in your reading doesn't take the place of knowing exactly what the word means. Get in the dictionary habit. Have a plan or a system for reading that includes writing words that you aren't sure about in a notebook—or looking up a particular number of words at the end of your reading. Keep your dictionary nearby so that you can get to it without looking all over the house, or going to someone else's room for it. Buy a dictionary written for high-school or college students. Try to develop an interest in words, where words come from, when they are used; find the synonyms (very similar to) and the antonyms (opposite of) of the word in order to learn the shades of meanings. These synonyms and antonyms are found in a thesaurus (Greek word for "treasury"). A paperback edition of *Roget's New Pocket Thesaurus* should be on your desk right next to your dictionary. A thesaurus is easy to use. It is arranged in dictionary form and it's a must for your writing. For instance, when you are writing a book report or term paper, instead of using the word "marvelous" four times, look at your thesaurus and choose other related words or similar words for "marvelous": wonderful, fabulous, spectacular, remarkable, outstanding, prodigious, prime, splendid, superb . . .

Reading develops vocabulary which develops ideas which enrich *your* life!

WHAT SHOULD YOU READ?

Most of you will have many teachers who assign all kinds of things to read so that you may never have to ask this question. Some of you, however, will have a chance to select your own reading materials from a list of assigned reading; and others of you will get no direction whatsoever for your reading.

Reading lists are only suggestions. A guide to your reading possibilities, rather than a rule about your decisions, is the intent of any reading list. The reading list included in this chapter was written for those of you who are going to college.

The National Council of Teachers of English is a professional group of English teachers from all over America who are concerned about what students read. They have published a list that was prepared by asking English professors of first-year college students what they think high-school students should have read before they got to college. The list is arranged alphabetically—not according to the most important books.

Some books are deleted and new books added as students react to what they have read and as teachers change. The best list available for the college-bound student is the following *Suggested Precollege Reading*:

SHAKESPEARE—PLAYS

1. *Julius Caesar*
2. *Hamlet*
3. *King Lear*
4. *Macbeth*
5. *Romeo and Juliet*

POETS

British

1. W. H. Auden
2. William Blake
3. Robert Browning
4. Robert Burns
5. Lord Byron
6. Geoffrey Chaucer
7. Samuel T. Coleridge
8. Thomas Hardy
9. Robert Herrick
10. Gerard M. Hopkins
11. A. E. Housman
12. John Keats
13. John Milton
14. William Shakespeare —Sonnets

American

1. e. e. cummings
2. James Dickey
3. Emily Dickinson
4. T. S. Eliot
5. Robert Frost
6. Allen Ginsberg
7. Langston Hughes
8. Robert Lowell
9. Marianne Moore
10. Edgar Allan Poe
11. Ezra Pound
12. Edwin Arlington Robinson
13. Theodore Roethke

British	American
15. Percy B. Shelley	14. Carl Sandburg
16. Alfred, Lord Tennyson	15. Walt Whitman
	16. Richard Wilbur
17. Dylan Thomas	17. William Carlos Williams
18. William Wordsworth	
19. William Butler Yeats	

PROSE

1–2 Suggested, above all others in this section, the Bible—at least a substantial portion of it—and Homer's *Odyssey*

3. Jane Austen, *Emma* and *Pride and Prejudice*
4. James Baldwin, *Go Tell It on the Mountain*
5. Samuel Beckett, *Waiting for Godot*
6. Charlotte Brontë, *Jane Eyre*
7. Emily Brontë, *Wuthering Heights*
8. Albert Camus, *The Stranger*
9. Lewis Carroll, *Alice's Adventures in Wonderland*
10. Rachel Carson, *The Sea Around Us*
11. Willa Cather, *My Antonia*
12. Cervantes, *Don Quixote*
13. Eldridge Cleaver, *Soul on Ice*
14. Joseph Conrad, *Heart of Darkness* and *Lord Jim*
15. James Fenimore Cooper, *The Pathfinder*
16. Stephen Crane, *The Red Badge of Courage*
17. Daniel Defoe, *Robinson Crusoe*
18. Charles Dickens, *David Copperfield, Great Expectations,* and *Oliver Twist*
19. Fyodor Dostoevski, *The Brothers Karamazov*
20. Ralph Ellison, *The Invisible Man*
21. Ralph Waldo Emerson, *Essays*
22. William Faulkner, *The Bear*
23. Henry Fielding, *Joseph Andrews*
24. F. Scott Fitzgerald, *The Great Gatsby*

25. Benjamin Franklin, *Autobiography*
26. William Gerald Golding, *Lord of the Flies*
27. Graham Greene, *The Power and the Glory*
28. Thomas Hardy, *The Mayor of Casterbridge* and *The Return of the Native*
29. Nathaniel Hawthorne, *The Scarlet Letter*
30. Joseph Heller, *Catch-22*
31. Ernest Hemingway, *A Farewell to Arms, Short Stories,* and *The Sun Also Rises*
32. Hermann Hesse, *Siddhartha*
33. Homer, *Iliad*
34. Victor Hugo, *Les Miserables*
35. Aldous Huxley, *Brave New World*
36. Henry James, *The Turn of the Screw*
37. James Joyce, *A Portrait of the Artist as a Young Man*
38. John Knowles, *A Separate Peace*
39. Malcolm X, *The Autobiography of Malcolm X*
40. Herman Melville, *Billy Budd*
41. Arthur Miller, *Death of a Salesman*
42. Mythology—Bulfinch's or Hamilton's collection
43. Eugene O'Neill, *Long Day's Journey into Night*
44. George Orwell, *Animal Farm* and *1984*
45. Francis Parkman, *The Oregon Trail*
46. Alan Paton, *Cry, the Beloved Country*
47. Plutarch, *Lives* (selections)
48. Edgar Allan Poe, *Tales*
49. Ole Edvart Rölvaag, *Giants in the Earth*
50. Edmond Rostand, *Cyrano de Bergerac*
51. J. D. Salinger, *The Catcher in the Rye*
52. Bernard Shaw, *Androcles and the Lion, Pygmalion,* and *Saint Joan*
53. Sophocles, *Antigone* and *Oedipus Rex*
54. John Steinbeck, *The Grapes of Wrath*
55. Jonathan Swift, *Gulliver's Travels*
56. Henry David Thoreau, *Walden*
57. John Ronald Reuel Tolkien, *The Lord of the Rings*

58. Mark Twain, *Huckleberry Finn* and *Life on the Mississippi*
59. Virgil, *Aeneid* (especially books 2, 4, 6)
60. Thornton Wilder, *Our Town*
61. Tennessee Williams, *The Glass Menagerie*
62. Richard Wright, *Black Boy*

HOW DO YOU CHOOSE BOOKS FROM THE LIST?

Nothing is worse than trying to select a book for a required reading report by just picking a book by its title and knowing nothing more about it! It's making a decision on the basis of almost nothing. Again, the National Council of Teachers of English has prepared a paperback book, *Books for You*, to help high-school students with their reading selections. It is well worth 95 cents if you can't find it in your school library. It is an annotated guide to books for high-school students. An annotated guide means that it gives one or two lines of description about the book. For instance, if you select Jane Austen's *Pride and Prejudice* from the Pre-college List, *Books for You* describes it on page 15: "In this early nineteenth century comedy of manners, Mrs. Bennett's ambition was to find husbands, preferably wealthy, for her five daughters; but there were many crises before any of the girls reached the altar." Here is a description of Hermann Hesse's *Siddhartha*: "The search for communion and contentment within the framework of Indian mysticism is the subject of this moving, human statement first published in 1922." *Books for You* will help you to select books for required reading as well as for fun. If you can't find it at your local library, write to Washington Square Press, Simon and Schuster, 630 Fifth Avenue, New York, N.Y. 10020.

For those who aren't interested in reading and who are not going on to college after high school, there is a wonderful book that will end your search for the thinnest book possible for your required English class book report; it is called *High Interest, Easy Reading*.

The National Council of Teachers of English wrote this book for students who can read but just aren't interested. Even though these books are easy to read, they are written for high-school students. If your library doesn't have a copy of it, send 95 cents to Scholastic Magazines, Inc., 50 West 44 Street, New York, N.Y. 10036. Ask for the latest edition of *High Interest, Easy Reading*.

WHAT CAN YOU LEARN ABOUT YOURSELF THROUGH READING?

There is no limit! Every subject that interests you—such as chapters in this book about sports, sexuality, or drugs—is just a beginning compared to all the written materials you can find and read in depth about each topic. You can learn how others your age and from other parts of the country or world think and act and how they behave in the same situation. You can learn about travel and people and animals and projects and how to build a log cabin. And all the time you are reading you are learning about your reaction to things that sound like you, to things that don't sound like you, and your reaction to where you are in the range of topics you read about.

You can learn that it's not only you who have trouble explaining your feelings to others; it's not only you who are worried about what to do in the summer, or when you get out of high school, or what to do about sex. It's not only you who are concerned and consumed with all the things that you can't talk about, or when you do talk about them to your friends they don't know any more than you do about them.

Reading brings to you the whole world of other people's experiences and discoveries that you will want to be in on as you are in the midst of decisions about your own world of experiences and discoveries.

Tests Are One Measure

Douglas D. Dillenbeck, former editor of *The College Handbook,* is the executive director of publications for the College Entrance Examination Board. His work at the College Board has always reflected his first concern: the student—*you.*

Mr. Dillenbeck's instructive chapter about testing is information that you, who are always being tested, should know. He describes to you what testing is, the kinds of tests used in high school, your use of these tests, and what the scores will tell you.

Each test gives you just one piece of information about yourself—not the whole picture—and you should use every measure of your work to get the whole evaluation, even your *own* measure of your work.

Tests Are One Measure

BY DOUGLAS D. DILLENBECK

When the teacher tells the class there will be a test tomorrow, usually everyone moans and groans and carries on as if it were the end of the world. Most people are only half serious when they act that way about a test—it doesn't really bother them that much because they usually do all right on tests. Some people really mean it, though. Tests worry them. They're afraid they won't do well, or they may even fail. Then the teacher may criticize, other students may laugh (or sympathize, which is even worse!), and their parents may be angry or disappointed. It's no fun to have other people finding out about your faults or weaknesses. If that's the main thing you think about when someone mentions tests, you probably worry about them too.

There's another way to think about tests that has more to do with *your* learning. No matter what reasons other people may have for giving you tests, you can use them, too, to get information about yourself. That's always a good thing. The more you can know about yourself, the better you can figure out what kind of person you are and can become. Tests can show you that you have abilities you may not realize. They can also show you weaknesses that you aren't aware of. Either way, you're better off when you have a good measure of these strengths and weaknesses than if you don't know about them.

When you find out you're especially good at something, you can begin to think about the best ways you can use that ability. Most of the famous musicians, athletes, and other kinds of performers that you know about discovered their special abilities when they were no older than you. Most scientists begin showing their special interests and abilities quite young, too. Some writers have their first books published only a few years after they finish high school. It's not too early for you to be thinking about what you want to do and be. Tests can help you do this.

SOME KINDS OF TESTS

Most of the tests you take in school are made up by your teachers and given only to their own students. A teacher may say that tomorrow your class will have a test on the chapter you just completed studying in your textbook. Or maybe it's the end of the report period, and the teacher gives a test to help determine the mark you will get on your report card.

The other main kind of test is the printed kind that your school buys or rents from outside, called a "standardized test." These may be given to all the students in your school—or perhaps just the students in your grade—usually not more than once or twice a year.

Teacher-Made Tests

The test that your teacher makes up usually consists of a few questions or problems taken right from the material your class has been studying. It may ask you to remember certain facts, like important dates or the names of people or things, or it may ask you to write what you think about some subject, or it may give you certain problems to solve. After the teacher has marked all the test papers and returned them to the class, you can see how well you (and everyone else in the class) did on that test. This gives you two kinds of information about yourself. First, it shows how close you came to measuring up to the teacher's expectation. If your mark on the test is 80, it means you answered correctly about 80 percent of the questions that the teacher thought you should be able to answer. Or, if your teacher uses a different system of marks, you may get a mark of B, which usually is a way of saying that the teacher judged your test paper "good."

It's nice to know how well you are meeting each teacher's expectations, but you have to be careful about how you interpret that information. Do you know some teachers who seem to expect a lot from students and have the reputation of being "hard markers"? Their tests may be long and difficult, and very few of their students get high marks. Do you know some teachers who are "easy markers" and give out a lot of high marks? Most people have had both kinds of teachers by the time they reach high school. Because teachers give different kinds of tests—some easy, some hard— and mark them differently, too, you have to remember that your mark on a teacher's test is just *that* teacher's rating of your work—not anyone else's. A different teacher might have given you a test with easier questions, and you'd have gotten a higher mark. Which mark would be right?

The other kind of information you may get from a teacher-made test is how you compare with the other students in your class. If you know what marks the others got, you can see whether you were one of the highest, one of the lowest, or around the middle of the group. When you make this kind of comparison, it doesn't matter if your teacher is an easy marker or a hard marker, because you all took the same test and got marked by the same teacher.

You can't tell very much about yourself from just one teacher-made test, but after you have been in a class for several months and taken quite a few tests, you should begin to get a picture. Are your test marks

in this class *usually* around the average? Never mind
if an occasional mark is much higher or much lower.
Are your test marks in this subject usually higher or
lower than your test marks in other subjects? Are your
test marks in this subject this year generally higher or
lower than those you got in the same subject last year?
These are some of the ways you can look at your
teacher-made test marks for useful information about
you.

Standardized Tests

In some schools a student is given several standardized tests every year, beginning around the third or
fourth grade. In other schools, this kind of test may not
be used at all. Even if you have never taken one,
you should read about them, because you will probably
take some in the next year or so, and they may be very
important to you.

A standardized test is one that has already been tried
out on hundreds or thousands of other students to be
sure that the questions are clear and to find out how
hard or easy the test is. Most tests of this kind have a
lot of questions—50 or 100 or even more—but the
questions are short so you can answer them quite fast.

Very often the questions are "multiple-choice,"
which means that you just have to pick out the best
answer from four or five possible answers that are
given for each question. Here is an example of a
multiple-choice question: The opposite of *flexible* is
(A) soft (B) rigid (C) unsteady (D) angry (E)
fragile. The best answer is (B) *rigid*, because it comes
closest to meaning just the opposite of the word
flexible.

Standardized tests are often printed in booklets that
can be used over and over again. You are given a
separate sheet to mark your answers on— usually by
filling in with your pencil a space with the same letter
as the answer you chose. For example, you would

answer the question given above by filling the circle marked (B). If you haven't taken standardized tests before, you might be put off at first by these special ways of presenting the questions and recording your answers. You will get used to them, though, and then you'll be able to appreciate the convenience of being able to answer the questions by just making a pencil mark instead of having to write out a lot of words and numbers.

Usually your answer sheet will be sent somewhere else to be "scored" by a machine that can count your right answers and wrong answers with practically perfect accuracy. It may be a few weeks after you take the test before your school gets back a report and passes it along to you. By then it may be hard to remember what the test was like, but you should try, because that will help you to understand what your score means. (What you get on a teacher-made test is usually called a mark or a grade, but on a standardized test it's a score.)

WHAT SCORES TELL YOU

Standardized test scores come in many forms. They begin with some person or machine counting the number of questions you answered correctly and sometimes the number you answered incorrectly or didn't answer at all. These counts give your paper a number called a "raw score," which doesn't mean anything all by itself, so usually you don't even get told what your raw score is. For example, you might take a test with 96 questions, and you get a raw score of 62. If that's all you knew about how you did on the test, would you think you had done well or poorly? But now suppose you are told that only five ninth-graders in every hundred get a raw score as high as 62 on that test, and all the others—95 percent of all ninth-graders—get lower raw scores than that. Now what would you think about how well you had done?

The number 62 tells you nothing, but 95 percent

tells you a lot, and that is one way your score may be reported to you. It is called a *percentile*, and it tells you what percentage of some group of students you did better than. When your score is reported to you as a percentile, you always need to know what group it refers to, so you can say that you did better than, say, 95 percent of some particular group. It might be all the ninth-graders in the country, it might be all the students in your school who are taking ninth-grade mathematics, or it might be just the students in your school who are applying for a special class in college-level biology. In fact, your score might be compared with the scores of several different groups, and you would get a different percentile for each group.

Instead of a percentile rank, your score might be given to you in form of a *grade equivalent score*. This kind of score is used quite a lot with elementary-school tests in various subjects and skills, like reading and arithmetic. They are used in high school, too, sometimes, but this is harder to understand because students study different subjects in high school. You may have taken tests called "achievement tests" in elementary school, and you—or more likely your parents—were told that your mathematics score was "at the tenth-grade level." That sounds as if it means that you could do tenth-grade mathematics when you were only in the sixth grade, but you know that it couldn't mean that. What it really means is that you answered the questions on that test—mostly the kinds of mathematics problems that you had studied in the sixth grade or earlier—as well as the average tenth-grade student would answer them. That's not a very useful kind of information, but it may be the only kind of report you get from some tests. You can still compare your own scores with those of your classmates to get a general idea as to whether you came out high among them—or low— or around the middle. And you can use a simple rule to turn a grade-equivalent score into a similar comparison with students of your grade all over the country. If your grade-equivalent score is about the same as the grade level you are at, your score on the test is about average. Any higher grade-equivalent means above-average performance on the test, and the higher the grade-equivalent score, the further above average it is.

One other way that scores on standardized tests are often reported is called a *scaled score*. This just means that the raw scores on a test have been converted to numbers in a certain range or scale—usually so the scores on different tests can all be put on the same scale and compared with each other. Scaled scores, like raw scores, don't tell you anything all by themselves, so whenever your test results are reported as scaled scores, you will probably be given percentiles, too, or else tables in which you can look up various percentiles for your own scaled scores.

NORM GROUPS

This is a term you may hear or see when you are finding out how you did on a standardized test. It's important for you to understand it. The norm group is the whole population you are compared with when your score is turned into a percentile or a grade-equivalent score. Usually on a test of school ability or achievement, the norm group will be the girls and boys in your grade all over the country. Sometimes it will be just the boys (and a girl's scores will be compared with just the other girls' scores). Sometimes, especially if you are in a big school or a big school system, the norm group will be just the other students in your grade in your own school or city. Sometimes, on a test of interests—which may not be called a test, but instead, a questionnaire or inventory or preference record —your scores will be compared with those of adult men in different occupations.

Which norm group is used for comparison can make a big difference in how high or low your scores stand, so you must always know about the norm group in order to interpret your scores.

HOW OTHERS USE TESTS

Teachers and counselors use standardized tests not only to measure each student's abilities and school progress, but also to learn about the whole group of students in the school. They might find out, for example, that their seventh grade is falling behind the national population of seventh-graders in arithmetic skill, and they might decide to try to remedy this in the eight-grade mathematics classes.

Usually, though, such tests are given to help them learn more about individual students. A test can help them to understand someone's special learning problem, for example, by showing some weakness in a particular learning skill. A diagnostic test in arithmetic might show that you were fast and accurate in adding, subtracting, multiplying, and all other kinds of computation with the whole numbers but that you made mistakes almost every time you had to divide with fractions. Knowing this, the teacher could then concentrate on teaching you division with fractions and not waste time on other things at which you were already good.

Teachers and counselors may also use tests to identify your strong points and perhaps to plan special activities or classes to help you develop your best abilities even better. Teachers usually know your strengths and weaknesses pretty well after you have been in their classes for a while, but tests help them get to know you faster. They also help the teacher to learn to know you better if you're a very quiet student with special problems or abilities that would not be noticed in regular classwork and assignments.

TESTS FOR JOBS AND COLLEGE

When you apply for a job or for admission to college, you may be asked to take a certain test, or maybe a whole series of tests. The employer or college will use these, along with other information about you, in deciding how to answer your application. The employer wants to find out whether or not you have the ability to do satisfactory work in the job that you are attempting to fill. Or if there are several applicants, the employer may be trying to decide which one is best for the job. The college admissions officer, too, is trying to be sure that the applicant has the ability to succeed in that college. Or if there are many more applicants than the college has room for, the admissions officer may be trying to decide which ones are best qualified.

There are two other ways that many colleges use tests, and these may be very important to you someday. One way is for placement, or deciding what courses you would benefit from. A college might place you in a remedial class in English composition if your records, including certain test scores, seem to show that you needed to learn to write better. Or it might let you go right into a sophomore English course in your freshman year because you showed that you had already mastered the skills and knowledge that are taught in its freshman English course. When a college lets you skip over some beginning course and go right into a more advanced one, that is called *advanced placement.*

The other important use many colleges make of tests is to give credit for college work that you learned outside college. For example, if you are a good writer and qualify for advance placement in English, the college may also give you college credit for the freshman course it lets you skip. Some very able students who have learned college-level work in several subjects while they were still in high school find that they can enter college as sophomores and save a whole year's time and expense.

USING TESTS TO HELP YOURSELF

Even though you usually take tests only because someone else wants the information about you that they give—a teacher, a counselor, a college, an employer—it makes sense for you to use the information, too, for your own benefit. There will even be a few times while you're in high school when it will make sense for you to take certain tests just for your own use, even when they are not required by anyone else.

The main reason for this is that some tests are the best means available to get certain kinds of information that you need in making decisions and plans about your future. If you are thinking of going to a certain college and want to know how your scholastic abilities compare with those of the students who go to that college, the best way to find out is to take the same test of scholastic abilities that the students at the college have already taken and compare your scores with theirs. If you are trying to choose between two colleges and can make this comparison with each one, you may see that you would stand much higher in ability among the students at one of the colleges than at the other. That information may enable you to imagine some important differences in what it would be like for you at each college. This may be reason enough for you to choose one over the other.

As you go through high school, you may have the experiences of being high, low, and average in ability compared with the other students in various classes. You may find that one of these situations brings out the best in you. Perhaps you respond well to the challenge of having to work hard to keep up with the other students, who find the work easier than you. Or maybe you get discouraged in such classes but do your best work when you can have the satisfaction of being one of the best in your class. Or maybe it doesn't make much difference to you what the other students are like. How you react to situations may give you an important clue to how you will fare at college—and perhaps to something you should look into when you choose a college. Tests can help you do this.

One more way you may make use of tests for your own benefit is to build up a record of your academic achievement—especially if your high-school record, for some reason, is inadequate. Perhaps you lived abroad for some years and learned a foreign language that doesn't even show on your school record because you never studied it in high school. A test in the language might be the means for you to get it on your record that you have this skill, which you may want to be able to prove someday. Or perhaps you go to a school that is practically unknown to colleges because it's small or new or because very few of its graduates have ever gone to college. In any of these cases, a college admissions officer might not know how to evaluate your school record, not knowing how well you have been taught or what standards your marks represented. But your scores on familiar admissions tests provide useful additional evidence of your ability and preparation for college.

SOME TESTS TO KNOW ABOUT

Here is a list of tests you will hear about while you're in high school. As a rule, it will be up to you to decide whether or not to take these tests and when to take them, so it would be good if you knew something about them.

1. *Preliminary Scholastic Aptitude Test/National Merit Scholarship Qualifying Test (PSAT/NMSQT).* This test is given every October in most high schools, mainly for juniors, although anyone can take it who wants to. It's like the College Board Scholastic Aptitude Test (SAT) that hundreds of colleges require, so it gives you a chance to see what the SAT is like and how well you can do on it. It takes two hours, and you get two scores—a verbal score to show how good you are with words and language, and a mathematical score to show how well you handle numbers and quantities. You can compare your PSAT/NMSQT scores with the, SAT scores of applicants and freshmen at the colleges that require the SAT. They're published in a directory,

The College Handbook, which all high schools have for their students to use. If you take the PSAT/ NMSQT in your junior year, you will also be considered for the scholarship programs administered by the National Merit Scholarship Corporation.

2. *Scholastic Aptitude Test (SAT).* This is one of the admissions tests of the College Entrance Examination Board, required by about a thousand colleges of applicants for admission. It is given at test centers all over the United States and in other countries around the world on five Saturday mornings every year. Your own school may be a test center, or you may have to travel to the nearest test center at some other school or a college. The test takes three hours, and you get a verbal score and a mathematical score, like the PSAT/ NMSQT scores. Your school gets them, too, so they can help you with your plans for college. And your scores are also sent to the college or colleges that you ask to have them sent to. You can have them sent to colleges later if you don't know where you want them sent at the time you register for the test. You should take the SAT in the spring or summer of your junior year in order to get the most benefit from it. That way you get your scores early enough to use them when you're deciding what college or colleges to apply to. Also, if they happen to be lower than you think they should be, you still have time to take the SAT again and try for higher scores. If you don't take it in your junior year, though, you can take it in the fall or winter of your senior year, and that's early enough for most colleges.

3. *College Board Achievement Tests.* These are the other admissions tests of the College Entrance Examination Board, required by several hundred colleges. They are one-hour tests in fourteen high-school subjects, and as a rule you would take only two or three of them, depending on what was required by the college or colleges you were applying to. Some colleges give you a choice, and you pick the ones in your best

subjects. The Achievement Tests are also given at College Board test centers on certain Saturdays. Usually you wouldn't take any Achievement Tests before the spring of your junior year or winter of your senior year, but you might want to take one as early as the spring of your sophomore year if you were taking a subject that year—say, biology— that you would not take any more of in high school and you thought you might have use for a good test score in this subject.

4. *American College Testing Assessment Program (ACT).* This is an admission test of the American College Testing Program required by many colleges for applicants of admission. It is given at test centers throughout the United States and in several foreign countries on five Saturdays during the year. It takes about four hours, and you get scores in English, mathematics, social studies, and natural sciences.

5. *Advanced Placement Examinations.* These examinations in college freshman courses are offered by the College Entrance Examination Board and given by high schools to students who have taken special college-level courses in high school or learned the equivalent knowledge in some other way. Colleges may use your grades in these examinations to let you skip the corresponding freshman courses in college and even, in some case, to give you credit toward your college degree. In some colleges, a student who has gotten satisfactory grades on three or four of these examinations may enter as a sophomore and complete his undergraduate program in only three years instead of the usual four years. The examinations take a half-day each and are given during one school week each May.

6. *College-Level Examinations.* This is a program of examinations in college subjects, administered during the third week of each month at test centers throughout the United States and at military bases overseas. Although originally developed to serve adults

who needed a way to show colleges or employers that they had learned the equivalent of certain college courses in their work experience, by independent study, or by some other means, College-Level Examinations are being used by colleges more and more as a basis for granting college credit to incoming freshmen. If you have special knowledge of some subject that is commonly taught in colleges for credit, you might want to look into the possibility of taking the appropriate College-Level Examination and getting college credit for it.

TAKING TESTS WITH THE RIGHT ATTITUDE

Like most tools and instruments, tests can be used well or poorly, and their use can be helpful or damaging. The main thing for you to remember is that each test gives you just one piece of information about yourself—never the whole picture—so you should just add that information to everything else you know about yourself. If other information you have seems to contradict the test score—for example, if you get a low score on a test of something you've always been quite good at—the chances are that the test score is wrong. Don't believe the test score if you have better evidence of some other kind.

Even though you might get the impression that the purpose of tests is to keep you out of certain courses, programs, colleges, and careers, keeping you out is *not* their purpose!

If you think about tests with a healthy skepticism and remember that they are only one kind of measurement, you will see that there's no good reason to be nervous or fearful when you take a test. Tests aren't magic. They can't come up with answers about you or your abilities that aren't there. The more aware you are of your academic abilities and interests the less you will be surprised by test scores you get.

Think of your test scores as information about yourself, like your marks, teachers' comments, and your own interest in a subject—information that can help *you* make sound educational and career decisions. Information that will permit you to choose appropriate plans for your future.

Curriculum Choices

The purpose of high school is for you to find out exactly what you can do in different subjects and how well you can do it. Warren Farrell, author of *The Liberated Man,* has found that part of the difficulty young men have in choosing courses, majors, and careers is that they specialize too soon. Because of the competition for grades and colleges often the pressure to be on top results in studying only the things you do well in. If you do well in foreign languages, then you may feel you should not take science because it doesn't lead to a foreign language career. Or you specialize in science and decide not to take much foreign language. Or you specialize in mathematics and you decide against a general course in art. The same masculine mystique that says a young man must be in control, must be cool about it, and must be the great provider prevents you from choosing many areas of study that would broaden your range of interests and abilities if you would give them a try.

High school is the time to try everything. Specialization is for later. If you get a basic start in many areas of study, you will learn what interests you, rather than what others say "boys" are interested in.

Curriculum Choices

BY JOYCE SLAYTON MITCHELL

Curriculum is what educators think high school is all about. Curriculum means the courses or subjects offered in the high-school program. It is the reason to have high school, the core or heart of the school. It is the academic or educational part of your growth and development that the school is organized for. True, many high-school students would find a complete life without curriculum because of their time spent on and interest in sports, clubs, newspapers, music, cafeteria, and each other! All of these activities do keep students busy, and it is often easy to forget that curriculum or course work is supposed to be the central theme of everyday high-school life.

If you live in the suburbs or urban areas of America, it is possible to have over five hundred different courses to choose from as you plan your high-school program. As with all choices, the greater number of choices, the greater the difficulty to choose.

There are many ways to think about your high-school program. The most common way to select your course of study is to answer the often asked question, "What do you want to be when you get out of high school? A forester, an engineer, a medical technician, a lawyer, a social scientist?" With a career answer, the counselor then says, "You will need this course and that course," and your curriculum choice is all solved. Or you will answer the other question most often asked, "What college do you want to go to?" You will look at the college catalog, a general description of requirements will be listed, and once again, most decisions of subjects to study in high school will be made.

"Where are you going after high school?" or "What are you going to be?" become the counselor's questions to you rather than what program you will select in high school. Choosing high-school courses by what you want to be while still in the eighth grade can lead to many problems. The biggest problem is that you can't possibly know what you want to do when you don't know your options! And how can you possibly know your options when there are all kinds of things to be you haven't even heard of? And how can you know what you want to be when you have only seen a few different jobs compared to the many available, and you have talked to even fewer people in those jobs! What happens if you change your mind? Most of you will change your mind—not once but over and over again. As you grow and learn more about your academic abilities and your interests, you will change your idea of all things that are possible for you. That change is not taking place in a vacuum; the world of work, the types of jobs needed, and the employment and unemployment situation in the world are a rapidly changing situation.

Let's not take the most common way to go about choosing high-school subjects. Let's forget what you are going to do or be or where you are going to go five years from now. Let's concentrate on what you want to learn right now that will lead to your knowing a range of possibilities for your life. Let's plan a high-school curriculum so that the only doors that will be closed to you will be closed because of your ability and interests and personality. *Not* because of poor advice or poor planning.

HOW TO SELECT YOUR COURSES

What is the most logical way for you to select your high-school courses? Like all things in education, the future depends upon past record. The most significant way to choose your subjects for next year is by your school record and what you can learn of your test results. If you are in a school that groups eighth-graders or freshman English classes according to ability and you are in a top group, you will want to take the strongest academic program the school offers *regardless of what you want to be or where you want to go after high school*. If you are in the lowest group of eighth-graders, you will want to take a program that permits taking the very minimum requirements for continuing education after high school. If you are in the middle group of eighth-graders or of a high-school class, you will try what areas you can do well in and pursue those in depth. As soon as you find out that mathematics (Algebra and Geometry) or foreign languages aren't for you, take the two minimum years and go on to get more subjects in your stronger areas of study.

Even if you have your mind set on being an engineer, and you have a D in Algebra I and a D in Geometry, remember that requirements to be an engineer don't mean *taking* three or four years of mathematics, it means taking and having the ability to do *well* in three or four years of mathematics. Often career choices sound good because of what the picture of an engineer, or anthropologist, or social worker looks like in your mind, with little regard for your ability. Don't get stuck with the picture! Be flexible with your ideas of courses so that you are free to leave an idea after it proves not a good one, and you are free to go after an idea that is new because you have learned a new skill and interest. Chances are, with a D in two years of mathematics, or a D in French I followed by a D in

Spanish I, it isn't the teacher, it isn't that you didn't put in enough time. Those subjects just aren't for you.

If you are in a school where a teacher or counselor will discuss your test results with you, you will want to consider to some extent the results of your reading, language, readiness tests for Algebra, foreign languages, and achievement tests in certain areas. Most educators will agree that no decisions should be made on test scores *alone,* but they may show you that you have more ability than you have showed in your work and should give algebra a try. Usually, of course, your test scores coincide with your marks. When you are selecting eleventh- and twelfth-grade courses and have test scores that are much higher than your marks, chances are that you have already established your pattern of not studying. If you aren't terribly interested in schoolwork, then high test scores aren't very meaningful for predicting success in school. In other words, if by the time you are sixteen years old and you still use "not studying" as an excuse for poor marks, you should realize that you'll probably never enjoy studying as your major activity.

In addition to your past marks, test scores, and the help a counselor may give you in choosing your subjects, your teachers can be very useful in helping you decide what you can handle. Talk to your teachers when you can't decide whether to continue in a particular subject. The more ideas you can get about your work, the more information you will have for your final decision.

As you select your curriculum, always keep in mind the purpose of high school. Don't forget why you are there, and how curriculum fits into your life; it's you who are becoming a person and part of the person you are becoming is an educated and a thinking person. You are not in high school only because that's what teenagers do, but also because you want to find out exactly what *you* can do with your life and how well you can do it.

STRONGEST PROGRAM

What should a high-school program be like for a bright student who works hard and needs the strongest program available? A strong freshman program in a forward school (one where Algebra I and a foreign language begins in the eighth grade) will include English, Algebra II or Geometry, Biology, one or two foreign languages depending on the eighth-grade program, and a social science if a strong course is offered to freshmen or if it's required or if it's needed as a fifth academic subject.

English	Biology (or strong
Algebra II (or	science)
Geometry)	Foreign Language I
Foreign Language II	Social Science

Your choices in this program are which foreign language to study and whether to take Earth Science or Ecology if Biology isn't offered to freshmen.

A continuation of the strongest curriculum program would be:

Second Year:
English II	Foreign Language
Math III	Social Science (or
	one of options below)

Chemistry (or Biology or another foreign language)

Third Year:
English III	Foreign Language
Math IV	American History

Physics (or Chemistry or another foreign language)

Fourth Year:

English IV	Foreign Language (college
Math V (college	level)
level)	Foreign Language (or one
	of the options below)

Advance Placement Science (or Physics or Social Science)

In the above illustration the student will continue with a foreign language or social or physical science depending on how he or she does with previous courses, his or her interest in the courses, and the particular courses the high school offers. *These are not decisions to be made in the eighth grade,* but rather ones to be made after completing some work in these fields. They are also not decisions to be made on the basis of sex, so that boys should *know* that they can take and do well in foreign language as well as mathematics and social science as well as physical science. All bright students (male and female) should take four years of mathematics and four years of one foreign language or in-depth in all subjects when they are doing well simply to find out how well they can do in academic work.

If you have to choose between Mathematics IV or V or Physics, a good rule is to take the math. All college mathematics and physical science will be based on mathematics, so the more mathematical background you have from high school, the better understanding of science you can develop when you are in college. Most engineering colleges and physical science professors who teach college freshmen advise students to take mathematics if they must make a choice between physics and mathematics. However, most top academic students can take both.

FOREIGN LANGUAGES

There are so many options in foreign languages that often students can't decide which language or how many years of each to elect. Most educators agree that it is better to learn one foreign language in depth rather than two years of two different languages, as was advised years ago. For the strong academic student, however, keep in mind that the Ph.D. candidate must take a reading examination in two foreign languages, so that many feel a reading knowledge of two foreign languages is better than a reading and speaking knowledge of one language. For most students, the reading part is often overstressed in school. Students want to learn to talk and sing and communicate in a foreign language and not have to read the longest book list, as most foreign language is taught.

A basic question for students is whether to take a classical or modern language, which usually is a choice between Latin I and French I or Spanish I. Most language teachers would agree that, if you are going to take a classical and a modern language, that you begin with the classical language. If you have had no previous foreign language, you could begin with Latin in your freshman year and continue with it the next year. If you have started French or Spanish in the eighth grade, you can continue the modern language in your freshman year and begin Latin the same year. The rule that you begin only one foreign language at a time does have exceptions, and if you are especially good in languages and everything in your schedule works out best by beginning two foreign languages at once, then go ahead and begin them!

The decision you have to make about which modern foreign language to take is a difficult one because it is really a matter of preference rather than one of principle or best education. Usually you can choose among French, Spanish, and sometimes German, and less often Russian. If you live in Maine or Vermont and are close to French Canada, or in Texas or California and close to Spanish-speaking Mexico, or New York City with many Spanish-speaking people, it would make most sense to learn the language of your geographical heritage. If you begin one of the modern languages in elementary school, usually you would be best off to continue that particular language before starting another.

If you think that one foreign language is much easier than another, or you have trouble with French but have heard that Spanish is easier . . . *beware!* The only differences may be pronunciation. Learning any new language—learning the structure, verbs, and idioms of a different language—needs the same kind of regular study habits, the same understanding, and the same language ability. Who teaches the language will make more of a difference in how hard or easy the French or Spanish is than the language itself. Here again, if your high school is in rural America and offers only two years of Latin and French, or if you are an exceptional language student and all of the options of your school are not enough, remember you can get home study courses from accredited universities in Chinese, Russian, Hebrew, or college French.

SCIENCE

In talking about science programs, often the question arises about when to take the College Board Achievement tests in science. For instance, most students study biology in their second year of high school, and if they are considering using biology as a college board score, by all means they should take their achievement test in biology at the end of the year when they complete the course, even if it is in their freshmen year. It wouldn't be very valuable to the student or to the college to have a test score in achievement one or even two years after a course was completed.

MINIMUM COLLEGE PREP PROGRAM

Let's say you have the *worst* marks in eighth grade for anyone who wants to go on to school after high school; you are at the bottom of your class. Your test scores aren't good, but you think if you work as hard as you have this year, you could probably take the minimum academic program and pass. You want to continue your education at least to a two-year program, and you want to find out what you can do and what you can't do and where your interests lie.

The minimum requirements for continuing education in a college preparatory program will be four years of English, two years of higher mathematics (Algebra and Geometry), one lab science (Biology usually counts), and three years of social science.

There are also one- and two-year community colleges, trade, technical, and business programs beyond high school that will accept applicants with commercial subjects, and a general high-school program without Algebra.

For most two-year programs in a college, the following high-school program is necessary:

First Year:
English I   General Science
Social Science   elective

Second Year:
English II   Social Science
Algebra I   elective

Third Year:
English III   American History
Geometry   elective

Fourth Year:
English IV   Social Science
Biology   elective

Foreign language is not mentioned because many good schools in the country do not require a foreign language. If you have a hard time in English, and language is a problem for you, then foreign language is out of the question. If your language ability is fair and you are encouraged to take a modern language, then take Algebra I in the ninth grade, Geometry in the tenth, and foreign language in the eleventh and twelfth grades. *Do not take Algebra and a foreign language* together in your first year of high school if you are not a good student. If you do improve by the time you are in the eleventh grade, and it does happen, then take the foreign language at that time. Learning a total new language structure and higher mathematics requires more abstract thinking than your junior-high-school subjects have been. If you don't do too well with the concrete, don't plan to take the abstract!

Most high-school students will not take either of the programs illustrated because most of you will follow a program somewhere between these two extremes. Many subjects have not been mentioned that almost all students take: physical education, music and art, typing and business subjects, driver education, and trade and technical courses, depending on the type of school you go to and the part of the country you live in. These subjects all count. They interest you, you need a level of skill in physical education, typing, and fine arts, and the levels offered you vary from school to school.

Even though you write out a four-year program in the eighth grade, feel flexible and free to change it as you go along. Don't get stuck with an eighth-grade decision about how many years of science or foreign language you "need." What you really need is to know how well you can do these things. When you find this out, you can make your selection of subjects according to what you know about what you can do.

NUMBER AND LEVEL OF SUBJECTS

How many subjects should you take? The idea that you will make better marks if you take less usually doesn't work out that way. Most honor roll students take the most number of subjects. If you are an A or B student in the eighth grade, you should probably take five subjects; if you are less than that, maybe four academic subjects one year and five the next, depending on what the subjects are. Some of you will make that decision on the basis of other things you are doing—how many hours you spend in sports, in music lessons, in clubs, how many hours you work outside school, and how much time you spend sharing home responsibilities with your family.

Don't think that because your minimum requirements are satisfied by your senior year, you should take three academic subjects and elect art or driving or music in place of a fourth or fifth academic subject. The freshman year of college will be a full schedule, and it is important to prepare for this year by taking a strong senior year in high school. If you have been an A or B student, hang in there with strong academic subjects. On the other hand, if you have worked very hard and come through with a C average, the senior year is a good time to get the nonacademic courses that you haven't been able to think about before now.

If you have a chance to be in an advanced program and you wonder if you would be better off with a B in Advanced Chemistry or an A in the regular course, you will be interested in knowing that most colleges prefer a B in the advanced course. In addition to the grade, the teachers in the advanced courses are often more enthusiastic about planning their course, and the course usually has extras in equipment and priority in the school budget. Advanced courses often have many "hidden" benefits that would make them very much worth the extra effort on your part. If, however, advanced work makes you feel dumb and second-rate, it isn't worth your time. You won't be asked to join the class unless you have top academic qualifications. But it doesn't make sense for you to take a course that makes you feel like borderline intelligence, when really you are only borderline for an advanced group of students.

IT'S YOUR CHOICE!

Often your parents and teachers will disagree on what subjects you should take. The best thing to do in that case is to try to hear everyone's point cf view. As you listen to different ones giving their advice on curriculum, be sure to recognize their interest in the subject. For instance, a French teacher will tell you French is the thing, while a Spanish teacher will tell you Spanish is better.

As much as students would like to feel that the school, the counselor, or their parents are responsible for their high-school curriculum choices, the responsibility is really yours. You can't tell someone ten years from now that you didn't become what you wanted to because "someone" didn't tell you the best things for you. It is always your final decision to drop a course, to elect a new one, to try to change teachers, to take on extra work, to sluff off. All the advice from all the people who are quick to give you opinions will not be a substitute for your decision.

Select carefully, it's *your* high-school record we are talking about. Finding out what *you* can do educationally is what curriculum choices are all about.

An Art Choice

Arthur Montzka is a high-school strings teacher and a photographer. His chapter describes choices you can make in the arts. The sex-role stereotype for young men makes art a difficult choice because art is not one of the so-called masculine fields of study. Unlike the expressive artist, the masculine mystique does not permit you to express your feelings. Mr. Montzka writes from his experience as a student who specialized in science rather than music, because science was the "manly" thing to do. Finally, after a college major in science for two years and spending every spare minute in music, he switched over to major in music and has been happily employed ever since. Mr. Montzka's chapter will help you to see your art choices.

An Art Choice

BY ARTHUR MONTZKA

You are in daily contact with the arts in some form whether it be TV or radio, paintings or photographs on the wall, posters or books. You are an active participant in the arts if you sing, play an instrument, dance, act, or read poetry. Perhaps you are creatively involved through composing music, drawing, painting, or writing. There are many levels and depths of involvement in the arts. As an *appreciator* you can discover the highest forms of humankind's expression, as a *performer* you can interpret great works of art according to your own feelings about them, and as a *creator* of art you can find the highest level of expression within yourself.

YOUR CHOICES IN THE ARTS

As a male you have undoubtedly been influenced in your participation in the arts by views of parents, relatives, teachers, and peers, showing you what a boy is expected to do or not to do. The choices you have made so far may not be those you would have made had you been free of the various pressures and stereotypes thrust upon you. As a teacher working with students from elementary through university level, I see such pressures in operation daily. Academics and athletics are often stressed to such an extent that there is little time left for the arts.

Here are some common sex stereotypes concerning the arts:

"Boys should go out for sports; girls should participate in music and art."

"Boys should study architecture; girls should study interior design."

"Boys should play trumpet or drums; girls should play flute or harp."

"Boys can take part in the arts but shouldn't get too serious because they won't be able to make a 'decent' living; girls can afford to be serious about the arts because they will marry, raise a family, and will not have to worry about earning a living."

Such ideas have been around a long time and are with us today. These kinds of sex-role stereotypes will fade only through the work of many enlightened teachers and parents, but fade they must if each of you is to choose your own most rewarding path in the arts.

In addition to sex stereotypes there are many other factors that have probably had an effect on directions you have taken in the arts. Perhaps you have been limited in your choices by a lack of available opportunities. Many school systems still have minimal offerings in the arts. You may have joined a choir or studied an instrument not out of interest but because you wanted to be with your friends and not feel left out. You may have selected a field in the arts because you wanted to emulate a teacher whom you admired, or wanted to be more like a parent or relative accomplished in the arts. If there was lack of opportunity for you, it is regrettable; your desire to be with friends and do as your peers is understandable; and the desire to emulate teachers, parents, or relatives may not be bad. These factors all operate and are to a great extent beyond your control. But have they really resulted in your making the best possible choices for yourself? Not necessarily.

Your interest, aesthetic and creative needs, demonstrated aptitudes, and personality are main factors in your involvement in the arts. Hopefully by the time you are in high school you have already explored many areas of the arts and have found some that satisfy your artistic needs and are deeply involved in them. If there are other areas that you would like to explore but have not, whatever the reason, it is certainly not too late.

THE ARTS AS LEISURE

What can a serious involvement in the arts mean to you? As a leisure activity the arts can bring an enjoyment of beauty, an aesthetic meaning in life to balance what might be a bland life. If you are musical and have a nonmusic job, you might strum a guitar or play a piano for fun. Or to offset your nonartistic career, you might sing in a barbershop quartet, march in a drum and bugle corps, design and build fine furniture, paint landscapes, photograph flowers, write poetry, act in community theater productions. The list of possibilities is long. The important thing is that you are submerging yourself in an activity that balances your career and adds needed variety to your life.

You can work in the arts alone or you can enjoy, perform, and create with or for a group. Your involvement with the arts may take the form of an escape from society and be pursued entirely for your own satisfaction and self-discovery or it may be a direct and rewarding way of communicating with others. Most likely you would have a combination of the two. As an artist you might paint alone but then take great delight in showing your work to others at art exhibits. As a musician you could spend hours practicing on your own and playing for your own enjoyment but also play in an orchestra, play solos in church, play chamber music with friends, or give a recital. The arts are basically forms of communication, and communication on an artistic level is very rewarding. Close friendships with others interested in the arts will be an invaluable reward.

The teamwork and skill necessary for an ensemble performance in music, dance, or theater are akin to a team effort in sports. The adversary is not another team but is perfection. The group tries to give the most moving, spirited, precise, balanced, and alive performance of the work at hand. The success of the performance is judged not only by the audience or director, but also by the feeling each member of the group has toward his or her performance. No amount of audience appreciation will really help when the performers know deep down that they have given less than their best.

No two people in the audience will react to a particular performance in exactly the same way. In fact, one person may be utterly bored and another moved to tears by the same performance. It depends on what experiences, knowledge, and prejudices one brings with her or him, as well as the mood of the person or what other things might be on his or her mind.

THE ARTS AS CAREER

If you are presently a high-school student deeply interested and involved in the arts, you are no doubt wondering about this involvement in terms of a career. Should you try to find a job that uses your skill in the arts? Should you major in your particular artistic field in college and optimistically hope there will be a job waiting for you when you graduate, or should you size up the job market and tailor your college education to aim you toward a particular available job? These are important questions you must answer for yourself after weighing all possibilities.

Before pursuing a career in the arts, you must be highly motivated. The grueling work and practice necessary to become a fine artist, poet, writer, actor, photographer, dancer, or musician requires great dedication. And, though a "decent" living is definitely possible in the arts, the greatest rewards are in the art experience rather than financial.

The variety of professions in the arts is vast. Included are musicians, painters, sculptors, graphic artists, writers, poets, designers, salesworkers of materials for the arts, teachers in all art areas and at various educational levels. Explore all possibilities relating to your interests and abilities in order to come up with an occupation just right for you.

Perhaps of necessity, students majoring in the arts tend to be idealistic. In spite of the ever-changing job markets, it is wise to make *some* assessment as to the type of jobs available in your area of the arts and the extent of competition for them. Most art-related jobs are highly competitive regardless of the general economy. Also an assessment, as objective as possible, should be made of your present level of skill development and your potential for developing this skill to the required degree during college or other artistic training. Seek answers from those who work in your art field and from those who know your own development and potential and can give you an honest appraisal.

Investigate what training you need beyond high school and where this training might best be obtained. Is a college degree necessary? Can you acquire better training in a repertory company or as an apprentice to a master teacher or craftsperson?

Passing on your excitement and knowledge of art to others can be a most rewarding career. A large number of creative artists also teach. Many artists teach part-time or on temporary jobs to stabilize their income, and many more teach because of the pleasure gained in stimulating students in the arts. Teaching may take many forms: the one-to-one private lesson, conductors and their orchestra, college professors and their classes, the master and his or her apprentice. *Do* look into the possibilities in teaching as related to your specialty in the arts.

Whether practiced as career or leisure, an appreciation of the arts is something that will grow throughout your life. Gradual and continuous growth will enable you to enjoy ever more complex and profound works. A well-developed awareness of the arts will help you notice beauty all around you: the sights, the sounds, the smells. It will deepen your communication with others. It will help make a beautiful life.

EDUCATIONAL CHOICES

Out of High School

Learning by Correspondence

BY JOYCE SLAYTON MITCHELL

Correspondence (home study) is available to you from kindergarten through college. You may decide to learn by correspondence and take an advanced placement in mathematics, or an art course not offered in your high school, or to make up a failed Latin I course. You may decide to take a course in automechanics or selling real estate to get ready for a summer job.

The National University Extension Association and the National Home Study Council make available to you—upon request—lists of schools, colleges, and universities. The courses and programs from these two sources are approved by the U. S. Office of Education, just as your own school is approved.

Write for (1) *The Guide to Independent Study*, National University Extension Association, Suite 360, One Dupont Circle, Washington, D.C. 20036 ($1.00); (2) the free list of private home study schools and programs from National Home Study Council, 1601 Eighteenth Street, NW, Washington, D.C. 20009.

The University of London offers the only English-speaking recognized degree program with no residential requirement (you don't have to be on campus) to fulfill for a degree. For further information, write National Extension College, Shaftesbury Road, Cambridge, CB2 2BP, England.

Summertime Is Discovery Time

Here are summer ideas for camping, hiking, or biking; study or the arts; volunteer or paid work. Whatever your choice for this summer, it's a good time to try things related or seemingly completely unrelated to your school year. And it's especially a good time to discover that "it works" or "it doesn't work" for you. Use your summer experiences for one more input into your decision making so that you are *Free to Choose*.

Summertime Is Discovery Time

BY JOYCE SLAYTON MITCHELL

What are you going to do this summer? How can you spend your summer to learn more about what you are like? School vacation can be much more to you than a time off from school! It can be an independent time for learning, an independent time for trying things out that you have learned about your interests and abilities and future plans during the school year. It can be a time for a practical experience that gives you a change from your academic experiences.

Your summer choice may seem to be completely unrelated to learning in school if you choose to make money rather than grades your goal; or to volunteer in an unrelated area of interest from anything you have been interested in before, like volunteering in a hospital when your schooltime is directed toward a political career.

But nothing you do is unrelated to you. Everything you do—even the opposite interests from school interests—in work and play adds to your understanding of what you can do, how well you can do it, whom you like to be with, and how well you like what you are doing.

Whatever choice you make for this summer—travel, camp, hosteling, wilderness trip, community service, study, or selling—keep yourself open for the changes in your interests and attitudes. It's a good time not to get stuck with, but to test, an idea about what you want to do with your life. It's a good time to try. Try working with young children, raising money, surviving in the wilderness, working alone, working with scientists, or bankers, or volunteers, learning music with teenage musicians, singing with students from all over the country. And it's especially a good time to say, "I like it" or "I don't like it" or "There are some things I like about it" or "There are some things I don't like about it." And to use these reactions for one more input into your decision making.

The best choice or job in the world for your cousin or friend may be the worst choice for you! It's *your* choice and experience—not what someone else says it will be like for you. Trust your summer experiences and your reactions to them as you learn how they relate to your understanding of you.

To help you to think about ideas for your summer choices, use this list to begin planning your summer. Each category includes specific examples and addresses where you can write for more information. Most information is free; send for it if you are giving any consideration to that particular summer activity. Follow up other leads and suggestions and read the newspaper and magazine classified ads until something sounds just right for you. The more information you have, the better the basis for your decision.

CAMPING CHOICES

General Camps. A wide variety of sports and arts is offered in camps, usually for boys from six to fifteen years of age. Ask about special groups for your age. A good place to start to look for a camp, other than your friends, is the camp directory in *The New York Times,* and in *Parents' Magazine.* You can also write to:

American Camping Association, 342 Madison Avenue, New York, N.Y. 10017

Association of Private Camps, 55 West 42 Street, New York, N.Y. 10036

Special-Interest Camps. Many older teenagers go to a special-interest camp in art, music, hiking, aviation; sports such as football, basketball, tennis, or sailing; or study in science, oceanography, or conservation. Write American Camping Association for the addresses for special interests.

Work Camps. Work camps vary in their program from working all day to half a day's work with recreation, study, or religious activities for the balance of the day. Most of the programs are for both girls and boys and usually for older high-school students aged sixteen to nineteen. Many of the foreign work camps have a minimum age of eighteen years. Write to the organization that has most to do with your church/synagogue, Scouts, or YMCA/YMHA for possible work camp choices. Check first with your local church/synagogue, because the larger Protestant churches and Jewish groups have their own work camps. Write to:

American Friends Service, 160 North 15 Street, Philadelphia, Pa. 19102
Boy Scouts of America, North Brunswick, N.J. 08902
National Council of Churches, Room 704, 475 Riverside Drive, New York, N.Y. 10027
United Presbyterian Church in the U.S.A., Senior High Summer Program, 475 Riverside Drive, New York, N.Y. 10027
United Church of Christ, Summer Service Projects, Pottstown, R.D. 2, Pa. 19464
Lutheran Youth Ministry Work Camps, 2900 Queen Lane, Philadelphia, Pa. 19129
Protestant Episcopal Elko Lake Camps, 38 Bleecker Street, New York, N.Y. 10012
American Jewish Society for Service, Room 1302, 15 East 26 Street, New York, N.Y. 10010

YMHA, 1395 Lexington Avenue, New York, N.Y. 10028

Foreign Work Camps. Two clearinghouses for finding a foreign work camp situation are:

Vacation Work and Events Department, The National Union of Students, 3 Endsleight Street, London W.C. 1, England
Israeli Students Tourist Agency (work camps in kibbutzim), 2 Pinsker Street, Tel Aviv, Israel

More information about foreign work camps can be found in these books:

Workcamps, UNESCO, 1 Rue Miollis, Paris 15e, France
Working Holidays and Voluntary Service Abroad, 91 Victoria Street, London S.W. 1, England

HIKING AND BIKING CHOICES

Some of the nation's hiking clubs have special teenage chapters with hikes and backpacking planned just for them. Ask for teenage trips when you write to:

The National Campers and Hikers Association, 7172 Transit Road, Buffalo, N.Y. 14221
The New England Trail Conference, 629 Florence Road, Northampton, Mass. 01060
Sierra Club, 1050 Mills Tower, 220 Bush Street, San Francisco, Calif. 94104

Backpacking. At the following addresses you will learn about short and long trips for family and teenage backpacking groups:

Sierra Club, 1050 Mills Tower, 220 Bush Street, San
Francisco, Calif. 94104. Ask for the trips planned in
the U.S. region that interests you.
The Wilderness Society, Western Regional Office, 4260
East Evans Avenue, Denver, Colo. 80222. July and
August trips in all the national forests and parks.
For more information, send 25 cents for *Backpacking
in the National Forest Wilderness, a Family Ad-
venture,* Superintendent of Documents, U.S. GPO,
Washington, D.C. 20402.

Bicycling. The American Youth Hostel Association
is the only address you need if you are interested in
maps, tours, hostels, hosteling with groups on a tour,
or for touring alone. You must be fourteen years old
to tour in America and sixteen years old to tour
abroad. Write to American Youth Hostel Trips, 132
Spring Street, New York, N.Y. 10012.

WILDERNESS AND SURVIVAL CHOICES

Survival Schools. If you are 16½ years, write to:
Outward Bound, Isaac Newton Square, Reston, Va.
22070, for a list of its survival programs in the United
States. For other wilderness and survival camps, write
to The American Camping Association, 342 Madison
Avenue, New York, N.Y. 10017.

Mountain Climbing. The three choices listed include
instruction in mountain climbing as well as a major
climb as part of the experience:

Yosemite Mountaineering, Yosemite National Park,
Calif. 95389 (Alpencraft Seminar—five-day instruc-
tion to learn to climb).
The Alpine Club of Canada, General Mountaineering
Camp, P.O. Box 1026, Banff, Alberta, Canada
(two-week camp for over sixteen).
Canadian Mountain Holidays, 132 Banff Avenue, Box

1660, Banff, Alberta, Canada (The Young Explorer's Camp for ages twelve to seventeen, one-week sessions; the only camp especially for teens).

Canoeing. There are canoe camps for you to choose from or clubs that organize canoe trips such as the Boy Scouts, Sierra Club, American Youth Hostels, and the Appalachian Mountain Club. For specific information, write:

American Canoe Association, 1217 Spring Garden Street, Philadelphia, Pa. 19123
American White Water Affiliation, 456 Hawthorne, San Bruno, Calif. 94066
Maine Department of Economic Development, State House, Augusta, Maine 04330
Sierra Club for Canoe Trips, 1050 Mills Tower, 220 Bush Street, San Francisco, Calif. 94104

River Rafting. Most of the river rafting trips are in the West and are not organized for teenagers although some teens do go on these trips. Write for details about their hundreds of planned tours for the summer:

America River Touring Association, 1016 Jackson Street, Oakland, Calif. 94607
American Guides Association Wilderness Expedition, Woodland, Calif. 95695
The Sierra Club for River Rafting, 1050 Mills Tower, 220 Bush Street, San Francisco, Calif. 94104

Horseback Riding and Packtripping. Horseback riding trips are mostly in the West, usually for families, but some are planned especially for teenagers. Write to the following places for a list of their trips in the wilderness:

The Wilderness Society, Western Regional Office, 5850 East Jewel Avenue, Denver, Colo. 80222
American Guides Association, Woodland, Calif. 95495

The Sierra Club for Packtripping, 1050 Mills Tower, 220 Bush Street, San Francisco, Calif. 94104

TRAVEL CHOICES

United States, Canada, and Mexico. Organized groups of teenagers travel in hotel tours or camping tours as well as cross-country tours by bicycle. Camping, bus, hosteling, and sight-seeing tours planned especially for teens:

American Youth Hostels, 20 West 17 Street, New York, N.Y. 10011
Student International Travel Association (SITA), 50 Rockefeller Plaza, New York, N.Y. 10020 (tours for twelve-year-olds and over).
Boy Scouts of America, North Brunswick, N.J. 08902
Canadian Youth Hostel Association, 86 Scullard Street, Toronto 5, Ontario, Canada
Arista World Travel, 1 Rockefeller Plaza, New York, N.Y. 10020 (hotel tours for teens).
Fugazy International Travel, 342 Madison Avenue, New York, N.Y. 10017 (teenagers' hotel tours to Mexico and the West, including camping tours of the national parks).

See also Hiking and Biking Choices, Wilderness and Survival Choices.

Foreign Travel. To get abroad you may live with a family, go to a work camp, study abroad, hostel with an American group, or take regular sight-seeing tours. Some possibilities:

Council on International Education Exchange, 777 United Nations Plaza, New York, N.Y. 10017 (arranges low-cost student travel for individuals or groups and has available special student guides to all major cities).

220   *Joyce Slayton Mitchell*

American Youth Hostels, 14 West Eighth Street, New
York, N.Y. 10011 (inexpensive bicycle tours; must
be sixteen years old).

Experiment in International Living: sixteen to eighteen
years old; travel with a group and live with a family
for a month. Very popular program—apply early.
An intensive language training program in Vermont
is included. Write to: High School Programs
Abroad, The Experiment, Brattleboro, Vt. 05301.

Boy Scouts of America offers many international living
experiences to Senior Scouts. Apply to your local
leader for information.

Israeli Summer Institute: Cosponsored by the B'nai
B'rith Youth Organization and the Jewish Agency.
Write:

B'nai B'rith Youth Organization, 1640 Rhode Island
Avenue, NW, Washington, D.C. 20036

The Jewish Agency, Department of Education and
Culture, 515 Park Avenue, New York, N.Y. 10022
(several tours to Israel especially for high-school
students).

See also Work Camps in this chapter.

STUDY CHOICES

U.S. Study. Check first with your high-school teachers and with the guidance office for programs of study
to be found at local high schools, in local centers, in
community colleges, on college campuses as well as
correspondence schools and camps. Next, check school
directories in *The New York Times* and in *Redbook*,
and *Parents' Magazine* for summer schools. About
six thousand high-school students participate in a
National Science summer study program. Ask your
science teacher for appropriate programs for you.

See also Art Choices in this chapter, and the chapter,
"Learning by Correspondence."

Foreign Study: The two largest private organizations for high-school students' foreign study programs are:

American Institute for Foreign Study, 102 Greenwich Avenue, Greenwich, Conn. 06830 (about $1000 for a month at a university center and one week in London and Paris; live with family).

Foreign Study League Schools, 107 East 3300 South, P.O. Box 1920, Salt Lake City, Utah 84110 (American teachers, and orientation, dormitories with American chaperons, about $1000).

Other student foreign study programs are available from:

Council on International Educational Exchange, 777 United Nations Plaza, New York, N.Y. 10017

Scholastic International, 50 West 44 Street, New York, N.Y. 10036

See also Foreign Travel and the chapter, "A Foreign Experience: Study Abroad."

ART CHOICES

Art choices for teens can be found at camp, art centers, college campuses, private schools, museums, summer theaters, and in community programs. Check with your high-school teachers of art, music, and theater arts, and with the guidance office for local opportunities in the arts. Look at the summer directories in national magazines, for special camps for the arts. The two largest art centers and one campus offer music, art, dance, theater, creative writing, and filmmaking.

Chautauqua Summer School, Chautauqua, New York. An arts program includes a school of music, dance, art, and theater for fourteen hundred high-school students. It has a special spiritual emphasis, including sixteen Protestant denominational houses that offer Bible study and devotional services.

The Banff Centre School of Fine Arts, Banff, Alberta, Canada. Twelve hundred adults, college and high-school students meet for the arts above, plus ceramics, French, voice and opera, radio and TV production.

High School Fine Arts Camp, Arizona State University, Temple, Ariz. 85281

For music opportunities look in your local library for the March issue of *The Instrumentalist*, a magazine that lists hundreds of summer music programs for teenagers from rock to opera.

VOLUNTEER AND COMMUNITY SERVICE CHOICES

The first place to look for volunteer work is in your local church/synagogue, school, library, hospital, mental health clinic, or museum. Many of these institutions have established voluntary programs for teenagers, and others may find a project for interested students. There are two excellent lists of national volunteer services. Send for:

Invest Yourself, an annual pamphlet listing opportunities for voluntary service in the United States and abroad. Send 50 cents to The Commission on Voluntary Service and Action, 475 Riverside Drive, Room 665, New York, N.Y. 10027.

Everyone Can Help Someone as a Volunteer, a booklet with one hundred separate volunteer services. Write to National Center for Voluntary Action, 1735 I Street, NW, Washington, D.C. 20006.

The following agencies have teenage volunteer programs:

National Center for Voluntary Action, a government
agency, 1735 I Street, NW, Washington D.C. 20006

Ecology and Conservation Projects:

The Conservation Foundation, 1717 Massachusetts
Avenue, NW, Washington, D.C. 20036
Environmental Action, 1346 Connecticut Avenue,
Room 731, NW, Washington, D.C. 20036
Friends of the Earth, 529 Commercial Street, San
Francisco, Calif. 94111
Bureau of State Parks, Harrisburg, Pa. 17120 (in con-
nection with National Campers and Hikers Associa-
tion).
The Nature Conservancy, 1800 North Kent Street,
Arlington, Va. 22209

The Red Cross:

Check the Red Cross office nearest you for its programs in public relations, fund raising, blood collect-
ing, water safety programs, and disaster preparedness.

Social Action Programs:

American Freedom from Hunger Foundation, 1100
17 Street, NW, Washington, D.C. 20006
Adventure in Concern, 3802 Houston Street, San
Diego, Calif. 92101
The High School Project on the Robert F. Kennedy
Memorial, 3130 M Street, NW, Washington, D.C.
20007

National Park Service:

A government project that uses thirty-five hundred
teenage volunteers in the national parks each summer. Write: Office of Information, National Park
Service, U.S. Department of Interior, Washington,
D.C. 20240.

See also Work Camps.

JOB CHOICES

Most states require fourteen- to sixteen-year-olds to have a work permit or employment certificate verifying their age. This is almost always issued by your local school. Check with your guidance counselor, who will issue your permit or know where you should get it for the particular state where you want to work.

If you are not yet sixteen years old, your best bet for paid jobs is with young children, jobs around homes and with pets, maintenance work at summer camps, and some national park jobs which are open to fifteen-year-olds.

If you are sixteen years old, you can add to the list counselor or counselor-in-training at summer camp, national parks, ranches, resorts, hotels, restaurants, Federal Government jobs, and jobs in business and industry.

Look around home, ask your parents and their friends and your neighbors about possible jobs, use the local classified ads in the local and regional newspapers. Here are other ideas:

Home and Pets

House watching (water lawns and houseplants, check doors and windows daily for owners who are on vacation)

Home services (sweeping, lawn mowing, car washing, shopping, catering summer parties, bartending, driving, errands)

Painting (inside and out)

Dog walking

Pet sitting (feed, walk, check animals while owners are away)

Boarding pets

Young Children Jobs

Baby-sitting
Organize a baby-sitting service
Tutoring
Planning and organizing children's parties (birthday and holiday)
Planning and organizing children's recreation at home
Bible school or religious summer school teaching

Summer Camps

Working in kitchen and laundry for under sixteen-year-olds
Counselor jobs for sixteen- to eighteen-year-olds
Day camp, recreation, and church camp counselor

Information about boarding camp jobs is available at:

Boy Scouts of America, Recruitment and Referral Division, North Brunswick, N.J. 08902
YMCA Projects Director National Student YMCA, 600 Lexington Avenue, New York, N.Y. 10022
American Camping Association, 342 Madison Avenue, New York, N.Y. 10017
Association of Private Camps, 55 West 42 Street, New York, N.Y. 10036

National Parks

There are two types of jobs for high-school students in the U.S. national parks. About three thousand students from fifteen to eighteen years old work for the

Youth Conservation Corps (YCC). The work includes building trails, planting trees, and general ecological work. It is a government job and you can inquire and apply for a list of all the U.S. Youth Conservation Corps projects by writing: YCC, U.S. Department of the Interior, Washington, D.C. 20204. Then write directly to the national park for a job. Get your application in by January 1, since these jobs are very competitive.

The second type of job in the national parks is with private companies who run the park hotels, lodges, and stores. For a list of these private agencies, write to National Park Service, U.S. Department of the Interior, Washington, D.C. 20204.

Resort, Hotel, and Restaurant

Jobs in this field include busboy, dishwasher, salad-maker, hamburger clerk, tray-line worker, fountain clerk, pantry worker, host, waiter, kitchen helper, short-order cook, sandwich maker, carhop, cook's helper, bellboy, and cashier. Look in the classified ads, and in the travel and resort sections of the Sunday papers for places to apply for a job. Again, apply early. January and February are the months when the resorts hire summer help, and the early applications have the best selection of jobs.

Summer Theater and Fine Arts

High-school students have the best chance for a job locally. Ask your high-school drama, or art, or music, or English teacher for job ideas in summer theater or the arts. If there is a college or university near you, check with its theater arts, music, and art departments for possible summer jobs.

Government Jobs

There are some jobs in the Federal Government for the seventeen-year-old, and many state government jobs are available for sixteen- and seventeen-year-olds. The Postal Service hires students in the summer and for Christmas holidays. Check with your local post office for vacancies. Some special programs are created for summer jobs for students—write to your State Personnel Office and ask about its summer jobs for teens. The Highway Department usually hires extra students in the summer to work on construction.

Business and Industry

Summer help to replace regular workers on vacation is hired by your local banks, stores, business offices; and there are typing jobs, mailroom work, stuffing envelopes, bank teller trainees, messengers, and selling jobs.

If you are interested in a direct selling job, write for a list of businesses that will hire high-school students to sell their products: Direct Selling Association, 1730 M Street, NW, Washington, D.C. 20036.

Whether you are applying in person or writing a letter about your qualifications for a job, the facts employers are most interested in are:

Your training and work experience

Your willingness to work

Your maturity—regardless of your age

Your age—if you meet the minimum requirement for the job

The dates you have available for work

Good references about your character

Overseas Summer Jobs

Two booklets and four agencies are organized especially for student overseas jobs. The agencies vary in their services, from getting you a work permit only to getting you the permit, travel accommodations, and the specific job. Read *Summer Jobs in Britain*, Council of International Educational Exchange, 777 United Nations Plaza, New York, N.Y. 10017 and *Directory of Over-Seas Jobs,* Vacation Work, Ltd., 266 Ludlow Avenue, Cincinnati, Ohio 45220. Write:

Council on International Educational Exchange, 777 United Nations Plaza, New York, N.Y. 10017

Eurojob, 102 Greenwich Avenue, Greenwich, Conn. 06830

Vacation Work, Ltd., 266 Ludlow Avenue, Cincinnati, Ohio 45220

Worktrip, Young World, Mitchell Building, Milwaukee, Wis. 53202

Making Career Decisions

"What are you going to be when you grow up?" "A cowboy, a fireman, or an astronaut," replies the three-year-old boy, and adults don't stop pressing him about what he is going to be until he becomes a "something." In addition to the constant question, the elementary schoolbooks are filled with pictures of adult men continually at work. In fact, they are so hard at work that the impression that the first- and second- and third-grader gets is that the only purpose of life for a man . . . is to work. To be the great provider.

In the elementary textbooks, a father is seldom shown playing with his children, taking care of his children, relaxing with his wife, a partner of a working woman, or sharing domestic work in his home. Instead, he is racing through all the books working for pay. When boys finally get out of the sex-stereotyped elementary-school program and into high school, they are often counseled as if the purpose of their education is to transform them into an economic commodity. Their school years are organized into an economic investment concept which must bring maximum profit obtainable under existing market conditions. Young men's educational decisions are often programmed to lead to a society of big job seekers. The danger of being a society of big job seekers is that it creates the myth that says that the big job equals big money equals big man equals happiness.

Dr. Robert E. Gould, professor of psychiatry, says that in our culture money equals success. And for men, money equals masculinity. We can readily realize this fact when we think of the horror many young people have with the thought that a wife may earn more money than her husband. If a man were measured by any other way than how much money he earned, then no one would care which spouse earned the most money—everyone would be happy the family had two people sharing the financial responsibilities!

It is enough to frighten any young man when he realizes how much everyone measures a man by what he does for work and how much money he makes. How can you choose a career and make it feel like a natural developmental process when everything about your future career looks as if it is your only identity as a person?

Making Career Decisions

BY JOYCE SLAYTON MITCHELL

Many adults expect you to be completely responsible for your choices regardless of the amount of information you have in making the choice, regardless of the quality of information you have, and regardless of your personal understanding of that information. If you can learn how to choose—and if you can learn how to decide, then you will be better equipped to handle your career opportunities whenever they come. And you will be better able to decide the life-style *you* want your work to be in. Decision-making skills are the crucial necessity for the ever-changing careers and life-styles you can choose.

One way to solve a problem about what you are going to do is to get your focus off the outside pressures and to refocus on you. You don't have to concentrate on the prejudices and sex-role stereotyping of students, nor the school's expectation for you, nor career education, nor the world of work, nor the inflated economy that scares the life out of students, nor the changing labor market. All of these things will enter into what you actually do, *but* what you need most right now is to learn the skill that will help you to choose no matter what the conditions and changes are. And that skill is your ability to make a decision.

The first step in decision making is to define the problem you are making the decision about. Decisions are based on what you know and what you want. The decision-making process involves using what you know (or can learn) to get what you want. After you define the problem, you collect information on all of the alternatives for solving the problem. Then you choose one alternative. You take the alternative and look at all its possible consequences—at its advantages and disadvantages. All of your information must be related to you on a personal level because you are the one who has to take the responsibility for your choices. You are the one who makes the decision and who has the control—not someone in school, or at home. You are the one who enjoys or suffers the consequences of your decisions. Good decision-making skills will teach you to be clear about what information you need, to be able to figure out and estimate the possible outcomes of your decisions, to be clear in what actions you would take to reach these goals, and to be able to evaluate whether or not you did reach them.

Go through each of your alternatives in the same way. Be aware of the risks and costs involved in each of the alternatives. Notice how your situation, your values, and your goals fit into the alternatives. Then finally, develop a plan of action, a strategy to carry out your decision, to achieve your goal. You have great potential for making decisions and you can *make* your life happen as opposed to just *letting* it happen if you become aware of your decision-making possibilities.

Often, as you are thinking about career decisions, all of the things that you don't know seem to jump out at you—like you don't know what the employment opportunities will be, you haven't heard about a lot of careers, you don't know if you'll be married or if your wife will be working or if you would be supporting a wife and baby, you don't know how much time you will want to spend working for money, and you don't know how free you will be to travel.

Let's look at what you do know. You do know that you are probably going on to some kind of higher education or you are in a vocational program right now. You know your school record.

Your past record is always the best place to start when you want to judge or make decisions for where you are headed. After all, school is your work, your present career. As you consider what you know about yourself, look at your school record and take an inventory. Include in this inventory your grades, your extracurricular activities, your test scores, your ability to get along with other students, your leadership qualities, your persistence on class projects, your ability to get along with authority as represented by your teachers, your coach, and your parents. Include your interest in your homework and learning and your level of motivation and ambition.

Using all of the information you have about yourself, you can begin to think about your career and ways you want to spend your life. The particular subjects you like and do well with are a beginning for thinking about an occupation. Strong English, language, and verbal abilities can take you into reporting, publishing, or law; and fine arts abilities can take you into museum jobs, art, or acting careers. Strong mathematics and physical science backgrounds can take you into any one of the many careers in technology, medicine, the physical sciences, or business. Remember, too, that many occupations require a well-educated college graduate, regardless of his or her major. Personnel in these occupations are looking for an alert, responsible, good decision maker who can be taught the specifics that are needed while on the job.

Some students look at their school record and decide that they have had enough school and they want to train for a job right now and get on with it. At the senior-high-school level, vocational education offerings are found both in comprehensive high schools and in area vocational schools. Basic vocational skill training is being offered in an increasingly large number of areas—including health, agriculture, business and office occupations, food services, personal services, consumer and homemaking education, marketing and distribution, and trade and industrial occupations. But it is at the post-high-school level, especially in the rapidly growing numbers of community colleges, where the highest degrees of vocational skill are offered. This training prepares students to perform successfully as skilled craftspeople and technicians in the current occupational society.

Less than 20 percent of all the jobs in our country require a college diploma, and the numbers of unskilled jobs are declining, so you can see that most job opportunities are in the trade, technical, and business area. Vocational training is not only for those who can't go to college. It is also for you who want a special skill for earning money at a high hourly rate. One young college graduate who wanted to study his children's learning patterns at home took a course as an X-ray technician in order to work half time to bring in his share of the family income and have the rest of his time for his project. Vocational training is for all students who seek a job with good pay and flexibility in their work life, giving them time to spend with their family and/or other interests they choose for their own life-style.

Dr. Kenneth B. Hoyt, Director, U.S. Office of Career Education, has written some questions for students who are thinking about a trade, technical, or business career. He asks, "Are you the kind of person who

Has interest in *both* thinking and doing?

Really wants to learn things that will help you get a job?

Is willing to work hard in order to get a set of job skills?

Doesn't like to study unless you can see a direct tie-in with the kind of work you hope to do when you finish?

Has a pretty good idea of the kind of work you would like to do?

Likes to learn things that help you *do* something concrete and productive on your job after learning?"

If so, a vocational career rather than four years in college may be the very best thing you could do to get ready to work.

Your evaluation of yourself through your school record and extracurricular activities of publications, sports, fine arts, and clubs will give you a much clearer idea of your abilities and interests than any test devised to judge you. Remember, your record is your performance, not your potential, and this is what counts by the time you are sixteen, seventeen, and twenty-one. Without achievement, all the potential in the world is not likely to change at this point. If you haven't studied as much as you intended to in the last four years, chances are that you won't in the next four years.

Evaluating your needs and values is a little more difficult. Some basic questions that may help you to think about them are: Do you like to be with people? To work with a team or others your age? To work alone? With children? With the handicapped? Do you like to work with ideas, or with machines, with computers? Do you like to be in a complex situation and under pressure of deadlines, or in simple situations, planning each step ahead? A few questions that will influence your career and the types of jobs you choose will include: Do you prefer a particular situation or location, types of people with whom you will work, or is money the main goal? Do you think you will share domestic work and child-raising responsibilities with your wife? Will your wife share financial responsibilities with you? Do you think you would like a job that's short on money but long on prestige? Would you like a job where you can be left to work on your own?

The more you can think about your needs and values, the more information you will have for making your life decisions good decisions. After your self-inventory you are ready to start relating this information about yourself to the hundreds of jobs that are available to you. The first step is to read about the various careers with *you* in mind. Your accomplishments in school, your ambitions, your hopes, and a view toward the type of life-style that has most to do with you. As you read about different occupations and one sounds just right, write for more information, begin to look around for people in the same career to whom you can talk. Make an appointment with them and carefully plan your questions in order to use the time with them most effectively.

Read as much as you can about the careers that interest you. Remember that all of the career information must always be related to *you* and your understanding of yourself. When friends tell you the thing for a guy to be is to become an engineer because they are always in demand and the pay is great, it won't do you any good if you can't stand to do mathematics! Or if they say the thing for you to be is a long-haul truck driver, it doesn't do you any good if you can't bear to be alone. There is no such thing as one great career for all people, any more than only one right college, or school, or one right friend for everyone.

Once you get an idea that makes sense for you, use your summer-vacation time for a trial of your idea. Work on construction if you are interested in the building trades, or in a hospital if you are interested in a health career, with a children's group in a day camp if you are interested in education, in a political office if politics and community work interest you. Try a summer job in a bank or real-estate office if business is your interest. There are many summer job possibilities, and using this time to explore career interests pays off in experience and learning about your interests as well as in the money you make.

There are some things educators know about vocational development for students which may be helpful to you as you work on your career development. First, choosing a career is a long process rather than a choice out of the blue. You are selecting your career possibilities as you elect your curriculum in high school and college, if you take French IV in place of Mathematics IV. You made one of your biggest selections in career possibilities if you elected Algebra I in place of General Mathematics back in the eighth grade. As you choose a vocational program or a trade school or make your college choice, you are making career choices.

Second, there is no one occupation which is the only right one for young men. People have many career potentialities, usually related, where they can use all they have to offer and find satisfaction in their work. Third, most everyone compromises in his or her final career outcome.

Career experts say that the people who are happiest in their work are ones who get a chance to use everything they are and have an opportunity to handle as much responsibility as they are capable of handling. The main idea for you is to look at who you are and decide who you can become. The age-old story is that the career that pays the most in money or prestige is not a satisfactory way of choosing a career. You will want to choose a career because you are a talented, interested young man who has something to offer this world of ours in terms of your abilities, your time, and your values.

There are hundreds of jobs in many career lines which you should be aware of. There are many ways to do them—we must think of alternatives in time and people as well as alternatives in jobs. For instance, you may wish to share a job and use the rest of your time at writing, or growing grapes, or raising a child, or you may want to work part-time, or volunteer some of your time or create your own job. Dr. L. Sunny Hansen, Chairperson of Psychology and Counseling at the University of Minnesota, would encourage counselors to be creative in their questions to students about their work, and she says let's not ask, "Where do Johnny and Janie best fit?" but, "How do work and leisure fit into the kind of life that Janie and Johnny want and the kinds of persons they perceive themselves to be?"; not, "How can they be shaped to fit the labor market?" but, "How can work be shaped to individuals?"; not, "How can they be prepared to fit into jobs that now exist?" but, "How can they be prepared to help create jobs that need to be done to improve society and also fulfill their personal needs?"

In order to give you an idea of the range of possibilities beyond the usual career opportunities you have heard so much about, two careers lists follow. None of the careers listed under Vocational Careers requires more than two years of school beyond high school, while most of the careers listed in the College Careers require more than two years of higher education.

The first place for you to begin to learn more about any career that interests you is to look it up in the *Occupational Outlook Handbook*, published every two years by the U.S. Department of Labor. The *Handbook* should be available in your guidance office, or school library. If not, send $7.00 to buy it from Superintendent of Documents, U.S. Government Printing Office, Washington, D.C. 20402. Basic career information in the *Handbook* includes a definition of the career, the educational requirements, how many are in the career, where most people are employed, salaries, the future opportunities, and address of the professional organization where you can write for further information.

VOCATIONAL CAREERS

(Not more than two years of higher education required)

accounting technician
aeronautical and
   aviation technician
agricultural
   engineer technician
air-conditioning, heating
   and refrigeration
   technician
aircraft flight attendant

aircraft flight engineer
aircraft mechanic
airline pilot and copilot
airline traffic agent and
   clerk
applied arts technician
appliance repair service
   technician
automobile-body and

fender person
automobile, bus, diesel,
    and truck mechanic
automobile salesworker
bank clerk and teller
barber
bookkeeper
broadcasting announcer
broadcasting technician
business machine service-
    person
business office worker
carpenter
chef and cook
chemical engineering
    technician
civil service careers
coach
commercial artist
communications
    technician
computer programmer
    technician
computer service
    technician
computer operator
    technician
cosmetologist
data processing
    technician
dental assistant
dental hygiene
dental laboratory
    technician
drafting technician
electrical appliance
    service technician
electrician
electrodiagnostic
    technician

electronics technician
embalmer
engineering graphics
    technician
fashion careers
fire fighter
food processing
    technician
food service technician
forestry and wildlife
    technician
funeral director
home economics
    technician
hospital administrator
hospital attendant
hotel-motel restaurant
    manager
industrial designer
    technician
industrial engineering
    technician
industrial manager
    technician
inhalation therapy
    technician
insurance agent
insurance claims adjuster
institutional management
    technician
instrumentation
    technician
interior design and
    decorator
keypunch operator
laboratory technician
library assistant
machinist: all-round
machinist: tool and die
    maker

marine technician
mechanical engineering
  technician
medical assistant
medical laboratory
  technician
medical records assistant
medical X-ray technician
military careers
model
newspaper careers
nurse, practical
nurse, R.N.
nuclear technician
occupational therapy
  technician
oceanography technician
optical technician
photographer
photographic laboratory
  technician
physical therapy
  technician
plumber
police and correctional
  technician
printing technician
psychiatric technician

public health inspector
public utility technician
radio and TV announcer
range manager
radiologic technician
recreation worker
real-estate agent
religion technician
respiratory therapist
  technician
salesworker
sanitation technician
secretary
social work technician
spacecraft and missile
  technician
surgical technician
surveyor
telephone craftsperson
textile technician
TV broadcasting
  announcer
TV broadcasting
  technician
travel agent
veterinarian's technician
welder
wildlife technician

COLLEGE CAREERS

(At least two years of higher education required)

accountant
actor
actuary
advertising careers
airline pilot and flight
  engineer

airline attendant
anthropologist
archaeologist
architect
army
artist

astronomer
automobile dealer and
  salesworker
banking careers
biologist
business executive
chemist
chiropractor
choreographer
city planner
civil service careers
clergy
college professor
college student personnel
  careers
commercial artist
computer programmer
conservation careers
copywriter
dancer
data processor
dean of students
dental hygienist
dentist
designer
dietitian
doctor
early childhood educator
earth science careers
ecologist
editor
education administrator
elementary-school
  teacher
engineer
fashion careers
Federal Bureau of
  Investigation careers
foreign language careers
Foreign Service careers

forester
geographer
geologist
geophysicist
group work
guidance counselor
high-school teacher
historian
home economist
hospital administrator
hotel-motel careers
industrial designer
insurance business
  careers
interior designer and
  decorator
interpreter
journalist
lawyer
librarian
magazine publishing
  careers
market research careers
mathematician
medical assistant
medical record librarian
medical technologist
mental health careers
merchandising
meteorologist
military careers
missionary
museum careers
music careers
navy
newspaper publishing
  careers
nurse
nursery-school teacher
occupational therapist

oceanographer
optometrist
Peace Corps
personnel careers
pharmacist
photographer
physical education
 teacher
physical therapist
podiatrist
police officer
political scientist
psychiatrist
psychologist
public relations careers
radio and television
 careers
real-estate careers
recreation careers

religious careers
rehabilitation counselor
secretary
social worker
sociologist
special education teacher
speech and hearing
 therapist
statistician
stockbroker
surgical technician
systems analyst
technical writer
travel agent
United Nations careers
veterinarian
writing careers
youth service careers
zoologist

Choosing Your College

There are many ways to go about selecting a college. One way is to go to the college closest to your home where you know the largest number of students. Another is to drift into the decision at the last minute and to go to the college that is recruiting the hardest for students. Many students select a college by a particular program offered, or career decision. The crucial question that all of you must consider as you select your college is, "Knowing who I am, what I can do, what my interests are . . . which colleges have the most to do with me, where I can make the most of who I am?" When you get as much information about the college as the college gets about you, then you will have the basis for a good decision.

Choosing Your College

BY JOYCE SLAYTON MITCHELL

The place to begin your search for a college is with *you*. It's not the college nor the university, but *you*, you need to know most about to make a good decision about where to go after high school.

Deciding not to worry about getting into college doesn't help. Just when you aren't thinking about it, a magazine or newspaper or TV program comes out with new student recruiting programs to get you interested, and there you are, thinking about colleges again.

The first thing you can do about colleges at the beginning of your high-school career is to learn what kind of a student you are. If you take the strongest program that you can handle well while in high school, you will learn how it feels to be the kind of a student you are. Some students work very hard and decide they really don't like it and choose a less competitive college or a program that is more practical than academic.

The next thing you can do during your first two years of high school is to listen and read whenever you hear someone talking about a specific college, and go to any programs your school has open to freshmen and sophomores for college information. Whenever you hear college representatives recruiting for the college they represent, make an effort to notice where the information is coming from. When your uncle tells you there is no place like Central U., remember, it was fifteen years ago that he was there. When a young man on your street tells you how unfriendly all the students are at Northern U., keep in mind that he didn't have any friends in high school either. So be sure you know who says what, and make an opinion about the source of information as well as the information.

There are many ways to select a college. One way is to go to the college closest to your home where you know the most number of students. Another is to drift into the choice at the last minute and go to the college that is recruiting the hardest for students. Many students select a college by a particular program offered, or because they have decided upon a particular career. Still another way to select a college is to make a systematic survey of all the universities and colleges available and to select a few that have the most meaning for you. When you get as much information about the college as the college gets about you, then you will have the basis for a good decision.

Too many students concentrate their search for a college on the basis of whether they can meet the admission requirements, or where it is located, or its tuition and living fees. These are certainly important factors, but it is also essential to understand in some detail what the college is like and if it is a setting in which you are likely to achieve success. You must ask more than, Can I get in? You must also ask, What will it be like after I get in? Only then can you begin to ask yourself, What are the implications for me of one type of college life over another type? Will I be different if I go to a collegiate-type college, or an experimental college, or a college for men? What effect will one campus atmosphere have on my selection of friends, of spouse, and on my religious, political, and career values?

A student choosing a college has much the same job as a college admissions officer selecting a student. From your record one can look at your height, weight, age, College Board scores, and marks, just as you can look at cost, location, programs offered, and requirements for admission to a college. However, until the admissions officer meets you personally and reviews personality reports from your high school, he or she doesn't have a precise idea of who you really are.

The many college guides on the market today will give you the range of options in higher education by describing each college. You can learn about enrollment, size of the community where the college is located, programs offered, cost, level of competition for admission, fraternities on campus, and campus life. The two basic and complete guides for you to look at are *The College Handbook*, edited by Susan F. Watts (College Entrance Examination Board); and *Comparative Guide to American Colleges*, by James Cass and Max Birnbaum (Harper and Row). In addition there are several good guides written by college students which you will like and that will give you a student's view of what the college life will be like. The best of these is *The Underground Guide to the College of Your Choice*, by Susan Berman (Signet Books). The best source for scholarships and financial aid is published each year and you can order *Meeting Your College Costs* free from the College Entrance Examination Board, Box 592, Princeton, N.J. 08540. It gives step-by-step directions for when and where to apply for financial aid.

The characteristics you need in a college will be the result of your past school record; your family background; the size of the community in which you grew up; your interests, abilities, and educational and career plans for your future. As you go through the college guides and find categories important to you, note the colleges that occur several times in your choices, and read many descriptions of the college by different sources to try to get a total picture. Some colleges will sound good immediately, they will feel right for you, while others will not. If your selections are limited to one or two colleges, go through your criteria again and be more flexible on some kinds of information in order to get as wide a range as you think would work for you at this time. Undergraduates should look at broad offerings in programs rather than at specifics. If you are interested in physical science, you may end up in some physical science but not necessarily in biology, which may be your main interest right now. If you are like most prospective undergraduates, you aren't quite sure what you want to be, or which program is best for you. If you do choose a program, chances are that you will change programs before you actually graduate. Many courses open to you at college are courses that will be completely new to you.

Reading about college life on a campus will give you an idea of differences among college cultures. When you compare the rules of various colleges, you will learn about their differences regarding student responsibilities and college authority. You will get an idea of campus character or personality. It should be clear that the campus atmosphere does not indicate the degree of academic competition for admission. You cannot tell how hard it is to get into a college by the number of hours the library is open. Conversely, you don't have to be a superior student to find a college with an intellectual atmosphere and where much of the responsibility for his or her work is given to the student. And the opposite is true. Many colleges that take only above-average and superior students have a very collegiate rather than intellectual atmosphere, and with little academic or social responsibility given to the students.

Whatever the rules of the campus, you must relate them to your expectation of college. Look for the type of campus life you think will be most successful and most productive for you. Find a culture or setting that gives you an opportunity to try out your interests and abilities. Choose a setting that gives you the kind of support and encouragement that you need. If you don't have a sister, and have few female friends, you may find that coed living makes you too uptight to cope academically. You must relate your findings about the differences in college life to yourself. Your findings

have no meaning for anyone else. You can see that
some of your friends would want and need a very different type of setting than you want. Ask yourself, "To
what degree can I take academic and social responsibility?" "How much responsibility do I take now for
my life?" "How strict are my parents in their rules in
relation to the college rules?" "In what kinds of classroom climate do I work the hardest?" "How do the
colleges that I am looking at relate to what I know
about myself and the degree of responsibility that I
take?"

These questions must be seriously considered as you
look at colleges and make your choices, if you want
an idea of what a college will be like *before* you get
there!

Not often mentioned for your college selection plan
is the fact that, after you decide the ideal type of college for you, you must also make a second, third, and
fourth choice. Sometimes you must settle for your third
and fourth choice, so make those choices as acceptable
to you as your first choice. You often have to learn the
meaning of compromise on a public or visible level for
the first time. Until this time in your life, your compromises and disappointments didn't have to be known
to quite as many people. Your grades may have been
a little lower than you had hoped, or you may not
have had as good a place on the team as you had in
mind. But you didn't make public your expectation as
you must with college applications. The college acceptance, rejection, or wait list is seen by friends,
teachers, and parents.

The social visibility of your college choice presents
many problems to everyone. One of the most compli-
cating factors is that you and your parents may not
agree with what group or subgroup you want to be
identified. For you, Reed College sounds just right,
but your parents feel a liberal campus will hinder their
status in the community, and they want you to go to
Middlebury. You often waver back and forth between
wanting the college you want and wanting your
parents' approval; you know you can't have both.

If you are clear about the kind of college you think would be ideal for you, most effective for you, you will have little difficulty making your first choice. The trouble comes when you are looking for your second and third choices *within* your ideal type that have different levels of academic competition for admission. Many students would rather switch their criteria for selecting the college with the best environment and program for them than to violate their self-image and go to a third- or fourth-choice college they have never heard of.

For instance, a senior selects Amherst as his ideal college. The counselor suggests Wesleyan (Conn.) for a second choice, Trinity (Conn.) for a third choice, and Bowdoin as the last choice. If the student isn't from the East and hasn't heard of Trinity or Bowdoin, he doesn't like telling people that he may go to one of them even though the atmosphere, values of the college, and percentage of liberal arts students going on to graduate school are very similar to his first choice. The one big difference in the four colleges is the academic level of competition for admission, and for intellectual work. He decides to apply at Boston University and Ohio State, because everyone knows those colleges.

All of a sudden the student has gone from "What is the best place for me" to "Where can I get in that looks good to me, and to people I care about?" You are giving all the reasons why a certain type of college and education are best for you, and then you completely disregard these reasons in order to find a visibly acceptable college. Your self-image counts. The social visibility of your college choice counts. But you must deal with aspects of your choice and get them together. You must try to see a relationship between you and your college applications.

Select a first right, and a second and third right. Representatives from colleges are a good source of information for you. Don't let them get all the facts as if their purpose of recruitment is more important than you finding out about their college. The college admissions scene has drastically changed to the student's advantage. For the first time in American education, people are questioning the value of everyone's going to college. Read Caroline Bird's, *The Case Against College* (New York: Bantam, 1975), for another point of view about college. Ask questions—questions that concern you, not necessarily the college's latest idea of what students want to know. Knowing you as you do, you can't fit into someone else's idea of education for you and spend your high-school years in preparation for their concept of education. Look at all the possibilities and ask, "Knowing what I do about me, what colleges are best for me?"

A Military Choice

The military offers a great variety of opportunities for career training and education. For many students it is the only place where you can get paid, all living expenses, and a guarantee of job training.

But as good as the educational opportunities are, you must be warned that the military carries on its training within a particular environment—the masculine mystique at its extreme. The military is the place that promises to "make a man of you." And what they mean by a man is a physical achiever. A person who learns and uses and values violence and aggression in order to win at all costs. It's the place that puts you down in order to teach you to put down someone else—the enemy. The enemy is often described as women as well as the Vietcong or Southeast Asians or other appropriate non-Americans.

Betty M. Vetter, Executive Director, Scientific Manpower Commission, writes about the multieducational opportunities in the military. She also gives you detailed information about the pay, allowances, and benefits; aspects of service life and the military environment; and cites two resources especially for high-school students where you can get more information.

A Military Choice

BY BETTY M. VETTER

When the military draft ended in June 1973, several million young men breathed a sigh of relief. Although the legislation for the draft is permanent, draft calls cannot be reinstated without specific action by Congress, and such action is not expected unless the United States gets into a war. However, you are free to choose whether or not you would benefit from a few years in military service, and whether that might lead you toward a lifetime career.

EDUCATIONAL OPPORTUNITIES

All the branches of the military services offer excellent educational opportunities, both for formal academic training at both undergraduate and graduate levels, and for training in specific skills provided in military service schools in everything from cooking to electronics. Most, but not all, of the skills taught by the military have a counterpart occupation in the civilian world, and most training received in military schools is transferable to civilian jobs. Some colleges give academic credit for certain courses successfully completed in military service. Most colleges and universities provide opportunity for students to bypass required academic courses in which they can successfully demonstrate proficiency by taking the College-Level Examination Program (CLEP) tests. These tests allow students to earn up to thirty credits in freshman courses.

The military services also provide for a complete college education at little or no cost to students who are enrolled in ROTC programs or in the military academies at West Point, Annapolis, Colorado Springs and New London, Connecticut. Graduates are committed to serve specified periods of time in the officer corps of the service which provided or paid for their education.

Project Ahead is a new army-student plan that allows college credits earned in the army to apply toward a degree. The army will pay up to 75 percent of the course tuition. Courses can be completed in night school on the army base or through correspondence courses. An adviser at the college (eleven hundred colleges are participants in this program) helps the student with his educational planning while he is in the army.

Another college option is education partially paid for by the government after completion of active duty. Since the Second World War military veterans have participated in a program such as the G.I. Bill. However, today's beginning enlistees cannot be sure that there will be legislation providing such educational benefits to veterans by the time they leave the service, since such bills traditionally have applied to wartime rather than peacetime service.

Taking college courses while in service is another alternative offered by all of the military services, depending on the availability of such courses to the individual serviceman at his duty station. In addition to courses taken at nearby colleges and universities, many servicemen and women have had an opportunity to complete credits for a college degree while in service, through correspondence college programs offered all over the world by American universities to servicemen and their dependents. Such courses are available through all the services, with the army providing undergraduate educational programs at all major army installations, both overseas and in the United States.

For those students who decide to enlist before finishing high school (a practice the military discourages), opportunity is provided by the services to participate in a program called PREP, where remedial, refresher, or deficiency courses may be taken prior to entering a post-high-school program. The chance to work toward and complete a high-school equivalency certificate also is available in all the services.

Army service schools provide training in more than three hundred specific skills, and the other services also offer training in a wide variety of skills. These include professional, technical, and managerial occupations; clerical and sales specialties; service jobs such as steward and fire fighter; farming, fishery, forestry, and related occupations; bench-work occupations, structural work occupations; and a set of miscellaneous occupations ranging from transportation services to bookbinding. The military service schools also provide advanced training in occupations unique to the military, such as infantryman.

ENLISTMENT

Enlistment in any of the services is open to men or women age seventeen to thirty-five who are U.S. citizens or immigrant aliens admitted for permanent residence, provided they can pass required physical and mental examinations. A high-school diploma or equivalent is desired by all services, and is a requirement for some options.

The period of enlistment generally is four, five, or six years, and enlistees are guaranteed a variety of options under different plans for which they can qualify. These include cash bonuses for training and assignment in the combat arms, and in certain noncombat critical skills required by the services; and guarantees of training in one of over three hundred specific skills for which you can see if you qualify by taking a test before you sign up. Options also include a choice of unit and a period of guaranteed stabilization, as well as a choice of service location for at least part of your service.

PAY, ALLOWANCES, AND BENEFITS

Pay is good—particularly for young men just out of high school who have no specialized skills. In addition to board, room, clothing, medical care, and the privilege of using the post exchange for purchases, beginning recruits receive $344.10 per month with fairly rapid increases. Under specific circumstances, an enlistee can move up to pay grade E-5 in as short a period as twenty-one months, to a monthly basic pay of $430.80. In addition, you will be provided basic allowances for quarters and subsistence if government quarters are not provided; receive incentive pay for hazardous duty; proficiency pay for serving in critical military specialties, or in certain special duty assignments; special pay for sea duty in the navy or for serving in certain foreign places where extremes in climate or inadequate facilities and services are experienced; special pay for diving duty; and for being subject to hostile fire. At the time of enlistment, you can get an enlistment bonus of up to $3000 in certain designated skills, and amounts varying from six months of basic pay to $12,000 as reenlistment bonuses.

You will earn leave at the rate of 2½ days per month as well as disability and survivor benefits. Free full medical and dental care is available, and additional allowances in both base pay and benefits are made for dependents. Upon completion of enlistment, some are entitled to veterans benefits, including education, hospitalization, insurance, loans, and some preferences in employment.

SOME ASPECTS OF SERVICE LIFE

You may already have heard about most of these inviting aspects of service life from recruiters either at your high school or at local recruiting offices. You may also have heard from older brothers, friends, or relatives some things about military life that are less appealing. You will have formed some opinions of military life through watching movies and television programs—none of which reflects all of the truth, but all of which reflect some of the truth about military life.

Some aspects of military life will be appealing to some but not to others. These include a rigorous physical training program during the seven-week period of basic training required of all enlistees. The military services are highly disciplined, and leave little room for individualism if it is in conflict with military regulations. Regulations will determine the length of your hair, the way you make your bed and store your possessions, the time you get up and the time you go to bed (as well as when you eat, when you are free to leave your base, when and how you must draw your pay, when and where you will be assigned to duty, and how you will carry out that duty). With few exceptions, once you have signed an enlistment contract with one of the services, you must carry out that contract to the end even if you find that the military life does not appeal to you, or you will face the problems of dishonorable discharge or fugitive status, which will adversely affect the rest of your life.

The military life certainly is not ideal for everyone. One of the most painful parts of the draft was the requirement that men serve whether they worked well in the atmosphere of the military or not. Most young people feel a sense of gratitude and indebtedness to their country, and are happy to serve it in some capacity; but some would prefer to work for their country outside the confines of the military.

Because of the necessary structure of the chain of command in the military service, there is a strong "class" system built into the military. The line between enlisted men and officers is a strong one which will be an irritant to some young persons, although it is considered essential by the military. Officers and enlisted persons do not socialize together (they have separate clubs); they do not live together (housing is provided for both groups, but not the same housing); and usually they do not eat together, although they may share common kitchen facilities and eat the same food. They work together, but with distinct separation of their authority. Orders given by officers and noncommissioned officers to men below them in rank must be obeyed, whether they seem sensible or not.

Enlisted men are not usually encouraged to think for themselves. There are rules and regulations to cover almost every facet of both professional and private life in military service, and you will be expected to know and follow them. This is a very comfortable situation for some people, since it is almost always possible to know exactly what is expected of you. It can be restrictive to others, who would prefer more leeway to choose for themselves how to live some aspect of private or professionl life. Or it can be a tremendous burden to some who work best with very little outside direction.

If you are learning to know who you are and under what conditions you can work and live most comfortably, you will be able to judge for yourself whether a hitch in one of the military services is likely to be useful to you. Millions of young men have gone through military services—most of them successfully, and most have benefited from such service, whether it was short enlistment, or a career. A few have found the military life intolerable and have chosen the very unrewarding path of desertion to escape. These make up a small proportion of all men who have served in the military, but thoughtful evaluation should prevent you from becoming one of them.

The opportunities for education available through

the military services at almost any level are marvelously good, and are limited only by your own ability and determination. Men in service do not have to worry about losing a job, joining the unemployment ranks, or wondering how to support themselves. The service has traditionally offered an opportunity for travel abroad, for enrichment of life experiences, for opportunities to do and see and participate in things the servicemen could not have experienced without such opportunities.

If, at this stage of your life, you feel uncertain about what career you would like to pursue, you may find that a few years in military service will point the way toward a choice you want. Service activities may give you a boost on the way to attainment of that choice. If you have been in school for twelve years and would like to do something else for a while before beginning more schooling, the military option is worth considering.

How can you find out about the details of the various options open to you in each of the services? Perhaps the best way to start is with two publications that should be available through your high-school guidance office or library. *Report—High School News Service* is a monthly publication of the Department of Defense, available to you at no charge: write High School News Service, Great Lakes, Ill. 60088. The publication is designed especially to inform high-school students of their responsibilities, benefits, and opportunities in the Armed Forces of the United States. The other publication, *Military-Civilian Occupational Source Book,* provided by the Department of Defense in cooperation with the Department of Labor, emphasizes the relationships between military and civilian occupations. It lists the names of military occupation specialties in each service that correspond to civilian occupations with which you will be more familiar. The first edition of this book, issued July 1975, is available free from Armed Forces Vocational Testing Group/RDX, Universal City, Tex. 78148.

If your counselor does not have these two reference

sources, send for them yourself. They are free. These two sources will clarify the distinctions among the services to help you decide what you most want in training and opportunity.

After examining these documents with some care, you probably will want to talk to a military recruiter for one or more of the services to get more details on a program you are interested in. Don't hesitate to ask for information, since recruiters are anxious to help you find the opportunity you want. However, remember that a recruiter's job is to enlist men, and it is not his business to tell you anything about those parts of the service which you might not find inviting.

Before signing any contract for military service, take time to review the program you have selected with one or more adults who know you well and whom you trust. These may include your parents, your counselor, a teacher, or any other person who knows enough about you to help you choose whether you would respond well to life in the military service.

Contracting for four or more years of your life is a big step, and should not be taken lightly. It could also be the first step on a long and satisfying career, so don't throw the option away just because it requires a commitment of fairly long duration.

If you believe military service might be a good place for you, think about whether you prefer to take advantage of military programs to complete college before entering the service as an officer, or entering the service before going to college. You may not want to go to school any more at all, and are looking instead for training in a field that will provide you with a career you can enjoy and learn to do well.

You are free to choose this option, as most young men before you have not been free to choose. You owe it to yourself to examine it carefully, before you decide one way or another.

A Foreign Experience: Study Abroad

BY JOYCE SLAYTON MITCHELL

If you want a foreign study experience, it does not have to be planned and selected by your high school or some special group. You can plan your own experience. You can choose to join other American students who are enrolled all over the world in foreign-university-level programs, nondegree programs, high-school programs, special programs for American students, summer programs, thirteen-year programs, or short-term programs.

The two organizations listed below will provide you with information you need about visas, passports, and exchange programs. They have brochures, pamphlets, books, and guides (many of them free), in addition to information about study for Americans in any country in the world. Be specific about where and when you want to go when you write and ask about study abroad to:

Council on International Educational Exchange, 777 United Nations Plaza, New York, N.Y. 10017. Ask for its free list of annual publications for high-school students, *High School Students Abroad* (50 cents), *Student Travel Catalog*, free, and *Youth Travel Abroad*, free, *Whole World Handbook*, a very complete list of opportunities for student travel, work, and study abroad, easy to read, and the best of its kind ($3.50). Get an application for the International Scholar Identity Card ($2.00), especially for high-school students traveling abroad, for discounts and free admissions while traveling.

Institute of International Education, 809 United Nations Plaza, New York, N.Y. 10017

Joyce Slayton Mitchell

was born in Hardwick, Vermont. An education consultant in Vermont and former school counselor, she received her A. B. degree from Denison University and an M. S. degree from the University of Bridgeport. Ms. Mitchell is the author of several books including *Other Choices for Becoming a Woman: A Handbook to Help High School Women Make Decisions* (also published by Delacorte Press) and *I Can Be Anything*, and is a contributor to various publications including *Seventeen* and *Ms.* magazines. She lives in Wolcott, Vermont, with her husband and two children.